**Third Course**

# Developmental Language and Sentence Skills
# Guided Practice
## Teacher's Notes and Answer Key

- **Grammar**
- **Usage**
- **Mechanics**
- **Sentences**

**HOLT, RINEHART AND WINSTON**

A Harcourt Education Company

**Austin** · New York · Orlando · Atlanta · San Francisco · Boston · Dallas · Toronto · London

## STAFF CREDITS

### EDITORIAL

*Executive Editor*
Robert R. Hoyt

*Senior Editor*
Marcia L. Kelley

*Project Editor*
Eric Estlund

### Writing and Editing
Guy Guidici, Amber M. Rigney, *Associate Editors*

### Copyediting
Michael Neibergall, *Copyediting Manager;* Mary Malone, *Copyediting Supervisor;* Elizabeth Dickson, *Senior Copyeditor;* Christine Altgelt, Joel Bourgeois, Emily Force, Julie A. Hill, Julia Thomas Hu, Jennifer Kirkland, Millicent Ondras, Dennis Scharnberg, *Copyeditors*

### Project Administration
Marie Price, *Managing Editor;* Lori De La Garza, *Editorial Finance Manager;* Tracy DeMont, Jennifer Renteria, Janet Riley, *Project Administration;* Casey Kelly, Joie Pickett, Margaret Sanchez, *Word Processing*

### Editorial Permissions
Janet Harrington, *Permissions Editor*

### ART, DESIGN, AND PHOTO

#### Graphic Services
Kristen Darby, *Manager*

#### Image Acquisitions
Joe London, *Director;* Jeannie Taylor, *Photo Research Supervisor;* Tim Taylor, *Photo Research Supervisor;* Rick Benavides, *Photo Researcher;* Cindy Verheyden, *Senior Photo Researcher;* Elaine Tate, *Supervisor*

### Cover Design
Curtis Riker, *Design Director*
Sunday Patterson, *Designer*

### PRODUCTION
Belinda Barbosa Lopez, *Senior Production Coordinator*
Carol Trammel, *Production Supervisor*
Beth Prevelige, *Prepress Manager*

### MANUFACTURING/ INVENTORY
Shirley Cantrell, *Manufacturing Supervisor*
Amy Borseth, *Manufacturing Coordinator*
Mark McDonald, *Inventory Planner*

Printed in the United States of America

ISBN 0-03-066397-0

1 2 3 4 5 022 03 02

# Contents

## Chapter 1

**PARTS OF SPEECH OVERVIEW:**
**THE WORK THAT WORDS DO**

## Chapter 2

**THE PARTS OF A SENTENCE:**
**SUBJECT, PREDICATE, COMPLEMENT**

## Chapter 3

**THE PHRASE:**
**PREPOSITIONAL, VERBAL,**
**AND APPOSITIVE PHRASES**

## Chapter 4

**THE CLAUSE:**
**INDEPENDENT AND SUBORDINATE CLAUSES**

## Chapter 5

**AGREEMENT:**
**SUBJECT AND VERB, PRONOUN AND ANTECEDENT**

## Chapter 6

**USING VERBS CORRECTLY:**
**PRINCIPAL PARTS, TENSE, VOICE, MOOD**

## Chapter 7

**USING PRONOUNS CORRECTLY:**
**NOMINATIVE AND OBJECTIVE USES; CLEAR REFERENCE**

## Chapter 8

**USING MODIFIERS CORRECTLY:**
**COMPARISON AND PLACEMENT**

# Contents

# To the Teacher

The worksheets on the following pages are designed for students who should be capable of doing on-grade level English work, but who, for whatever reason, have encountered a grammatical skill or concept that they are having difficulty mastering. You can now intervene by selecting practice exercises designed to help the student master that specific grammatical skill or concept. You can then give the selected worksheets to that student as an extra assignment that complements ongoing class work. Of course, it is important that the student with the deficiency also continue to participate in the regular class work so that he or she does not fall further behind. Worksheets can be used as daily or weekly take-home assignments, or they can be completed during times of the day designated for personal study. Occasionally, a student's grammatical misunderstanding might be so specific that the problem could be solved in one worksheet assignment. Often, however, the worksheet assignments will be more extensive. In fact, some students may rely on the worksheets for continual support throughout the school year.

The worksheets can also be used in conjunction with composition instruction. When a student writes an essay that contains one-too-many errors in the possessive case, for example, you can merely staple a possessive case worksheet to the student's paper to be completed along with the essay corrections. This method allows you to individualize grammatical instruction while you continue discussing the principles of composition with the whole class. It also allows you to help your students see the interdependency of the study of composition and the study of grammar.

Beyond the immediate benefits to your lessons in grammar and in composition, the worksheets can help with the long-term goal of boosting scores on state-mandated tests. In this regard, you will likely discover that even strong students have an Achilles' heel. For these students you can select practice worksheets that will target a particular weakness.

Finally, after a student has completed the selected worksheet assignments and you are fairly confident that he or she has mastered the point of grammar (say, direct objects), it is important to publicly acknowledge the accomplishment publicly. For example, you may be teaching a lesson on adjective clauses. During your discussion, you could call on a student who has mastered direct objects, "Edward, does this adjective clause have a direct object?" Edward gets to demonstrate his new expertise in front of his peers and can feel that he is no longer somehow separated from the mainstream of his classmates. This method will also associate the worksheets in the minds of the students with something positive, rather than with a notion of punishment.

Although the concepts in the following worksheets are presented in a very basic and concrete way, students who are struggling may benefit from an additional step in the teaching process. I have found that when my students and I use a consistent pattern of questions and responses in our discussions of grammar, learning becomes easier. I have incorporated many of these patterns in the sections that follow.

In the following tips to the teacher, you will also notice that I have consistently used one line under the subject, two lines under the verb, parentheses around prepositional phrases, and arrows from all modifiers to the words they modify. I have found that this consistent systematic approach has worked especially well for students who

- have attention-deficit disorder,

- find logical reasoning difficult,

- are generally disorganized,

- find grammar too abstract to remember on a long-term or even a short-term basis.

The use of symbols (underlining, parentheses, and arrows) provides a visual cue that students can use to identify what they already know so that they then can more easily focus on what they don't know.

# THE SENTENCE

When I started teaching grammar many years ago, I tended to downplay this topic, thinking that just about everybody knew what a sentence was and could easily identify the subject and the verb. I was so eager to get on to the more sophisticated aspects of grammar that I failed to lay the proper foundation and, consequently, caused unnecessary confusion in my students.

Many of your students may know a sentence when they see one but may be unfamiliar with the vocabulary used to discuss sentences. Familiarizing students with the terms *subject, predicate,* and *verb* is essential since these are terms that will be used throughout their study of grammar.

## The Subject

I tell students that the **subject** of a sentence is who or what the sentence is talking about. I write a sentence on the board and then ask, "Who or what is this sentence about?" When someone answers correctly, I underline the entire subject with one line, emphasizing the consistent use of this marking system. If the student leaves out part of the subject, I remind him or her to include the subject's modifiers. Next, I ask, "Can anyone show me the main word in the subject, the one that, more than any other word, tells what the sentence is about?" When a student comes up with the answer, I write "*ss*" over the simple subject. So far, the sentence might look like this:

*ss*
The old road along the coast leads you to the beach.

## The Predicate

I explain that a **predicate** is everything that is said about the subject. Continuing with the previous sentence, I ask the class, "What is everything that the sentence says about *the old road along the coast*?" When a student answers correctly, I double underline "leads you to the beach." Then, I explain that, in the predicate, the main word is the **verb,** which tells most about what the subject is doing or being. When a student locates the verb *leads*, I write *v*

over it. Next on the board, I vary the sentence to look like this:

*v*
The old road along the coast is the best way to the beach.

I explain that here the road is not doing anything; the verb *is* just indicates existence.

Next, we turn to **helping (auxiliary) verbs.** I explain that helping verbs can be used with both action and linking verbs, and I give many examples of both. I have found it extremely useful to supply students with a list of helping verbs to memorize:

- These helping verbs will always have a main verb after them: *shall, should, will, would, may, might, can, could, must, ought.*

- These forms of the verb *to be* can be used as helping verbs as well as linking or state-of-being verbs: *be, am, is, are, was, were, being, been, become.*

- These forms of the verb *to have* and *to do* can be used as helping verbs as well as action verbs: *have, has, had* and *do, does, did.*

To help students find the subject and the verb, I first stress the importance of understanding what the sentence is saying. Students who are having trouble with this assignment should read each sentence three times before they begin. Then, I ask them to find the verb and underline it twice, not leaving out any part of it. Finally, we ask the subject question (who or what did that [or is that]?) and we draw one line under the answer to that question. It is important to include in the examples some imperative sentences, so that students can work with the understood "you."

Remind students to be on the lookout for interrogative sentences. These sentences often begin with a helping verb, followed by the subject, and then the main verb. For example, "Do you like pasta?" Also, encourage the students to say "subject of the verb" instead of "subject of the sentence" or just "subject." This repetition reinforces the students' understanding of the function of the subject.

If your students have studied prepositional phrases, remind them that the object of a preposition can never be the simple subject. Encourage students to "corral" these phrases by putting parentheses around them. Setting them off from the rest of the sentence at this point helps the students focus more clearly on the simple subject and verb.

## PARTS OF SPEECH

Learning the eight parts of speech is important for students because, with this vocabulary, a discussion of other grammatical concepts becomes more productive. However, students must understand that a word's part of speech is usually not rigidly fixed. I show students that the same word can be a different part of speech in a different sentence. The word *down* demonstrates this idea particularly well since it can function as five of the eight parts of speech.

### Nouns

Tell students that they can easily remember what a noun is because it begins with the letter *n* and so does the word *name*. A noun names something. A noun is anything you can talk about, including things you can't see, such as love, power, and happiness. Tell students that if they're not sure that a word is a noun in a particular sentence, to put *a* or *the* in front of the word, and if *a* or *the* makes sense, the word is probably a noun.

### Pronouns

I motivate students to think about pronouns by pointing out that we use pronouns without even thinking about them. When I give them the sentence, "I bought a pizza; the pizza had mushrooms on the pizza," they can immediately see the usefulness of pronouns. We intuitively prefer, "I bought a pizza; it had mushrooms on it." I show students that they already know how to use pronouns, although they may not understand what a pronoun is: it takes the place of a noun.

### Adjectives

Ask students to close their eyes and to picture a pile of books. Then, tell students that each of them probably has completely different books pictured in his or her mind, yet all of them are imagining books. Tell the students they are going to modify, or change, the image they have by adding adjectives to their books. Then say: "thick books." Then, "thick, green books." Then, "thick, green, leather books." Then, "these four thick, green, leather books." All these adjectives have made the noun *books* more specific, by answering the questions, *Which? What kind of?* and *How many?* Be sure not to omit the last example using a number because students may overlook the fact that numbers can be adjectives.

I encourage my students to draw an arrow from the adjective to the noun or pronoun it modifies. To reinforce the meaning of this visual, I tell students that an adjective is like a dog on a leash; it stays close to its master, the noun or pronoun it is describing. Remind students that adjectives are usually right in front of the nouns or pronouns they modify but that they can also follow linking verbs as predicate adjectives.

When you ask a student to tell you why a word is an adjective, encourage this pattern of response: "Because it's not just any old book, it's a green book." "Because it's not just any old dog, it's a shaggy dog." "Because it's not just any old shoe, it's a dirty shoe," and so forth. The repetition of this pattern, however absurd it sounds, effectively instills in the student's mind an understanding of how adjectives function.

### Adverbs

Adverbs seem to be the hardest part of speech for students to master. I ask students to be patient. Sometimes learning something worthwhile takes a little time.

After defining the term and giving a few examples of typical adverbs ending in –*ly*, I explain further that an adverb could be any word that answers the question, *How? When?* or *Where?* Continually stress these basic adverb questions. When you ask students why a particular word is an adverb, encourage them to begin their response with the words *because it tells* and then to choose from the questions *How? When?* or *Where?* to complete their answer.

I encourage my students to draw an arrow to the verb, adjective, or other adverb that the adverb is modifying.

I rarely go to the movies.

Rarely do I go to the movies.

I go to the movies rarely.

You can use a pair of sentences, such as the following, to model the distinction between adjectives and adverbs:

She is a *fast* runner.

She runs *fast*.

In both sentences, ask students: Does *fast* answer any of the adjective questions: *Which one? What kind? How many?* Or does it answer any of the adverb questions: *How? When? Where?* Encourage students to draw arrows from *fast* to the word it modifies in each sentence.

### Prepositions

First, have students memorize a short list of common prepositions, such as *at, in, on, by, for, from, near,* and *with*. Learning this short list enables students to set up a mental paradigm, which helps them identify new prepositions. Then explain that a preposition shows a relationship between its object and another word in the sentence. Have students hold a pencil in their hand. Then say, while you are doing the same thing with your pencil, "Place the pencil **on** your desk, now, **beside** the desk, **under** the desk, **against** the desk, **above** the desk; move the pencil **around** the desk." This kind of physical involvement helps the student understand what a preposition does.

### Conjunctions

The lesson on coordinating conjunctions seems to be an easy one for most students. (We will save the more difficult subordinate conjunctions for the lesson on adverb clauses.) I usually just remind students to be on the lookout for conjunctions when identifying subjects, verbs and prepositional phrases. A student who does not read a sentence carefully might be inclined to pick out just half of a compound subject, verb, or object of a preposition.

### Interjections

Since interjections are not grammatically connected to the rest of the sentence, they are the easiest part of speech for students to recognize. You may want to have your students memorize the short list of interjections given in the textbook.

## COMPLEMENTS

I explain that not all sentences will contain a complement. Some sentences don't need one. Some do. "I sneezed" makes sense all by itself, but "I hit" cries out for another word to answer *What?* or *Whom?* Tell students that this word that completes the meaning of the verb is a complement. It looks like the word *complete,* and that's exactly what a complement does: it completes the meaning of the verb. Remind students that they can help themselves recognize complements by underlining the subject once and the verb twice and by crossing out prepositional phrases.

## PHRASES

I begin by explaining that a phrase is a group of words used as a single part of speech.

### Prepositional Phrases

Review with students the list of common prepositions. Also, remind them that a preposition shows a relationship between its object and some other word in the sentence. Show students how an object of a preposition answers the question *What?* or *Whom?* when we ask the question in this way: First, say the preposition; then, ask *What?* or *Whom?* On the board, for example, write, "The pencil is on the desk." Then ask, "On what?" Give the answer, "The desk. *Desk* is the object of the preposition." Then, note that the answer to the question, the object, is a noun or a pronoun. Put numerous examples on the board, and in a relaxed atmosphere, check for understanding by calling on individuals to ask and answer the object-of-the-preposition question. Point out that a prepositional phrase begins with a preposition and ends with a noun or pronoun. It includes any modifiers that come between these two parts of speech.

I encourage students to place parentheses around all prepositional phrases. Parentheses here, as in math, indicate that the material within them functions as a single unit. The prepositional phrase (in parentheses) will work as an adjective unit or an adverb unit. I have found that "corralling" prepositional phrases into parentheses greatly facilitates teaching subject-verb agreement and helps to keep students focused on the basic structure of a sentence. Many students over the years have told me that this practice has been useful in helping them to read and understand other school subjects.

After students put parentheses around a prepositional phrase, ask them to draw an arrow from the phrase to the word it modifies. Using pairs of sentences such as the following helps students see the relationship between simple adjectives and adjective phrases.

The *corner* house is hers. [Adjective]

The house (*on the corner*) is hers. [Prepositional phrase used as an adjective]

In the same way, students can learn to see the relationship between adverbs and adverb phrases.

She walked *home.* [Adverb]

She walked (*to her house.*) [Prepositional phrase used as an adverb]

## Participial Phrase

Tell students that a participial phrase is a group of words that is used as an adjective. The main word in a participial phrase is the present or past participle form of a verb. To help students identify present and past participles, tell them to look for verb forms that end in *ing,* or *ed, n,* or *en.* Then, have students check to be sure the verb form is used as an adjective and not as a noun.

### Present Participial Phrase

To help students distinguish between participles used as verbs and participles used as adjectives, use a series of three sentences such as the following.

The frog is **jumping** on the lily pads. [verb]

The **jumping** frog landed in the water. [participle] (Point out to students that it's not just any old frog that landed in the water; it's the *jumping* frog.)

The frog, **jumping on the lily pads,** landed in the water. [present participial phrase, made up of the participle plus a modifying prepositional phrase] (Point out to students again the adjective function of the participial phrase [it's not just any old frog; it's the frog *jumping on the lily pads.*])

You may want to point out at this time that verb forms ending in *ing* can also work as nouns. These nouns are called gerunds, and students will learn about them at another time. Just provide a brief example: *Learning about gerunds* is fun! In this sentence the gerund phrase *Learning about gerunds* is a noun phrase, subject of the verb *is. What* is fun? Learning about gerunds.

### Past Participial Phrase

Similarly, we can use a series of three sentences to distinguish past participles used as modifiers from past participles used as verbs.

The branches were **broken** by the wind. (verb)

The **broken** branches lay on the ground. (adjective) [Point out that not just any old branches lay on the ground; they were the *broken* branches.]

The branches, **broken by the wind,** lay on the ground. (past participial phrase) [Point out again that it's not any old branches; it's just the ones that were broken by the wind.]

### Infinitive Phrases

When teaching infinitives, I remind the students that one of the characteristics of verbs is tense or time. Unlike a finite, conjugated verb, an infinitive has no time constraints binding it: it is infinite.

After explaining that an infinitive can function as an adjective, adverb, or noun, stress that students can determine how an infinitive is used by asking:

- Does this infinitive answer the adjective questions?

- Does it answer the adverb questions?

- Does it function as a noun, in one of the noun positions in the sentence?

### Appositive Phrases

To help your students remember the purpose of an appositive, you can put an equals sign above the first comma in the phrase to reinforce that the phrase equals or means the same thing as the noun or pronoun before it:

$$=$$

<u>Mr. Jones</u>, **my brother's teacher,** <u>is going</u> to Spain.

I remind students to think of the commas that come before and after nonessential appositive phrases as handles. They can hold on to both handles and lift the phrase right out of the sentence. A nonessential phrase is an interrupter; it doesn't really need to be there.

# CLAUSES

An effective mnemonic device for teaching clauses is a picture of an eagle with its claws outstretched. In one claw it clutches a placard with the word "subject" and in the other claw, a placard with the word "verb." The eagle swoops down on a sentence and grabs the subject with one claw and the verb with the other. Now it has a CLAUSE in its CLAWS! Use the fingers of both hands to make claws that "grab" on to a subject **and** a verb every time the class analyzes a clause. My students never seem to forget this image.

## Adjective Clauses

Adjective clauses are fairly easy for students to identify because most begin with relative pronouns. Encourage students to memorize these identifiers. You might want to explain that "relative" refers to how this pronoun relates back to a noun or pronoun in another clause and, thus, ties the adjective clause into that clause.

Be sure that students see the relationship between adjectives and adjective clauses. Use a pair of sentences such as the following to demonstrate the connection.

Our **Florida** <u>relatives</u> <u>are visiting</u> us. [adjective]

Our <u>relatives</u> **who live in Florida** <u>are visiting</u> us. [adjective clause]

To reinforce the concept that an adjective clause functions as a modifier, encourage students to draw an arrow from the adjective clause to the noun or pronoun it is modifying.

## Adverb Clauses

Adverb clauses begin with words called subordinating conjunctions. Tell your students that if they memorize a list of common subordinating conjunctions, it will be easy for them to identify adverb clauses. Warn students that several subordinating conjunctions can also be used as prepositions or as adverbs. Therefore, if there is no subject and verb after the subordinating conjunction, there is no clause, and what we thought was a subordinating conjunction is actually a preposition or an adverb.

Have <u>you</u> <u>eaten</u> tofu **before?** [adverb]

<u>We</u> <u>had</u> supper **before the game.** [preposition]

**Before** <u>we</u> <u>ordered</u>, <u>we</u> <u>asked</u> for some water. [adverb clause]

Using the three sentences above, point out to students the relationship of the adverb clause to the adverb and the adverb phrase. Encourage students to draw an arrow from the adverb clause to the verb, adjective, or other adverb it is modifying.

Once they learn about adverb clauses, I encourage my students to use them often in their writing, especially introductory adverb clauses. These clauses pique the curiosity of the reader and, consequently, make the students' writing more interesting: Starting a sentence with *When they found a small key* makes the reader curious about what might happen next.

# AGREEMENT OF SUBJECT AND VERB

This topic is often difficult for students because the idea of singular and plural verb forms is somewhat meaningless to them. It is important to explain that verbs aren't actually singular and plural, but they take a form that goes with a singular or plural subject.

I have found that the following method invariably works if you are consistent in having students do all the steps.

**1.** Cross out prepositional phrases that come between the subject and the verb:

One (of the pages) *was* missing.

**2.** When the simple subject is singular, whether it is a noun or a pronoun, substitute *he, she,* or *it* (any one of the three will work).

(She)
The girl (with the books) *is* my sister.

**3.** When the subject is plural, substitute *they.*

(They)
The reasons (for his success) *are* easy to see.

**4.** When the following singular indefinite pronouns are subjects, focus on the singular endings *one* or *body:* **one, every*one*, every*body*, no *one*, no*body*, any*one*, some*one*, some*body*.**

**5.** When the pronouns *each, either,* or *neither* are subjects, think *each* **one,** *either* **one,** *neither* **one.**

(Each **one**)
Each (of the students) *has arrived.*

**6.** Compound subjects connected by *and* take a plural verb form. Substitute the pronoun *they* for subjects joined by *and.*

(They)
The coach and his assistant *attend* every game.

**7.** For subjects connected by *or* or *nor,* look at the subject closest to the verb. If the subject is singular, substitute *he, she,* or *it.* If the subject is plural, substitute *they.* To make the process even easier, just cross out the other subject(s) and the *or* or *nor.*

(She)
The twins or my sister *has* my book.

(They)
My sister or the twins *have* my book.

**8.** *Here, there,* and *where* are almost never subjects. If a sentence begins with one of these words, look for the subject after the verb.

(They)
There *are* five women on the committee.

**9.** If the pronoun *you* is the subject, remember that *you* always takes a plural verb form, even when it refers to one person.

# MECHANICS

The rules of mechanics, grammar, and usage are interdependent. Therefore, it is sometimes difficult to come up with mechanics tips or tricks that don't require prior knowledge of grammar and usage. Telling students to use a comma between independent clauses joined by a conjunction always assumes that they can recognize independent clauses and conjunctions. One of the best times to bring up many of the following ideas is during discussion of the associated grammar or usage concept.

## Capitalization

Most students have no difficulty recognizing *Jennifer* as a proper noun and *student* as a common noun and are not likely to capitalize such words incorrectly. Some students, though, may have more difficulty applying that principle to inanimate objects. Creating a series of sentences such as the following can help reinforce the concept.

If I had a boat, I would name it

_____.

A series of sentences like the one above could also be used as additional practice in using italics and quotation marks with titles. Students may be more engaged in learning to capitalize and punctuate names that they have come up with on their own.

## Commas

An earlier tip suggested that students think of the commas that come before and after nonessential appositive phrases as handles that can lift the phrase right out of the sentence. This image of commas as handles works equally well with any other nonessential elements. Write a sentence such as the following on the board, with the nonessential clause written well above the rest of the sentence.

**, which had been hopping from branch to branch,**

The bird

began to build its nest.

Alternatively, write the sentence above on strips of paper, one strip for *The bird,* one strip for **,** *which had been hopping from branch to branch,* and one strip for *began to build its nest,* and have a student or two students pull the nonessential clause out by the handles (the commas.)

## Spelling

Because rules for spelling are so numerous (and exceptions can seem even more numerous), students may get discouraged by seeing every one of their spelling errors marked in red. For students who misspell many words, you might suggest that they use a spellchecking program or keep a dictionary handy. Concentrate classroom instruction on words that a spellchecking program might overlook, such as *there, their,* and *they're.* If students can master such commonly confused words, they may feel better about having to reach for a dictionary to find the plural spelling of *thesaurus,* for example.

## CONCLUSION

These worksheets can benefit struggling students by helping teachers intervene before problems become crises. Because they are relatively easy to administer and evaluate, they can benefit overworked teachers. However, this strategy is only one of many that are available to us, such as using sentences from students' favorite books, magazines, or songs to model grammatical structures, playing quiz-show grammar games, singing, chanting, or rapping out grammar rules or lists, and allowing students who have mastered a point of grammar to tutor those who are having difficulty.

In teaching grammar, we should also take some time to consider the image of ourselves that we present to our students. For example, we might encourage our students to see us as a coach who is teaching them to field the grammar issues they encounter in their writing, but we must eschew any kind of image that suggests a dry-as-dust pedant or the grammar police. We can avoid the negative images if we remember what we are, and are not, trying to do. We are not trying to teach our students to be petty about errors, nor are we trying to get them to look down on those who speak non-standard English. Rather, we seek to empower students by helping them master basic language skills.

*Adapted from* Sentence Surgery: A Systematic and Graphic Method of Grammar Instruction *by* **Michèle Beck-von-Peccoz.** *Copyright © 2000 by Michèle Beck-von-Peccoz. Reprinted by permission of the author.*

On the following pages are quick reference charts that you may wish to copy and distribute to your students.

# SUMMARY OF PARTS OF SPEECH

| Part of Speech | Use | Examples |
|---|---|---|
| noun | names | **Shane** is playing **soccer** in the **park.** |
| pronoun | takes the place of a noun | **She herself** said **that all** of **us** have been invited |
| adjective | modifies a noun or pronoun | **This rare Roman** coin is **valuable.** |
| verb | shows action or a state of being | Shelby **is** the candidate who **will win.** |
| adverb | modifies a verb, an adjective, or another adverb | I jogged **nearly** five miles **today** but I think I ran **too fast.** |
| preposition | relates a noun or a pronoun to another word | Some **of** the streets were closed **on** Friday **because of** flooding. |
| conjunction | joins words or groups of words | **Either** Brandon **or** I will meet you **and** Darla at the airport **so that** you won't have to take a taxi. |
| interjection | shows emotion | **Hooray!** We're home! **Well,** we'll see. |

# SUMMARY OF PARTS OF A SENTENCE

| Parts of a Sentence | Questions to Ask | Examples |
|---|---|---|
| Subject | Who or what is the sentence about? | After lunch, the **members** of the drama club will be taking group pictures. |
| Verb | What is the subject doing? or What is the subject's state of being? | The slamming door **startled** the birds in the front yard. **Are** you excited about the recital this evening? |
| Predicate Nominative | Which word completes the meaning of a linking verb and identifies or refers to the subject? | Joseph Ferdinand is the **chairperson** of the volunteer committee. |
| Predicate Adjective | Which word completes the meaning of a linking verb and describes the subject? | The dogs were **thirsty** after their daily walk. |
| Direct Object | Which word completes the meaning of an action verb and answers the question *Whom?* or *What?* after the verb? | The principal gave each new teacher a welcoming **gift.** |
| Indirect Object | Which word answers the question *to whom?* or *to what?* (or *for whom?* or *for what?*) in sentences with direct objects? | The principal gave each new **teacher** a welcoming gift. |

# SUMMARY OF SUBJECT-VERB AGREEMENT

A verb agrees with its subject in number.

    (1)  Singular subjects take singular verbs.    *(The **cat sleeps**.)*

    (2)  Plural subjects take plural verbs.    *(The **cats sleep**.)*

    (3)  Compound subjects joined by *and* take a plural verb.    *(The **cat and** the **dog are** sleeping.)*

    (4)  When compound subjects are joined by *or* or *nor*, the verb agrees with the subject nearer the verb.    *(The **cats** or the **dog is** sleeping. The **dog** or the **cats are** sleeping.)*

---

When the subject follows the verb, find the subject. Then make sure that the verb agrees with it.

    *([Is, Are] the cats sleeping? The cats [is, are] sleeping? The **cats are** sleeping. **Are** the **cats** sleeping?)*

---

When a sentence has a verb phrase, the first helping verb in the phrase agrees with the subject.

    *(The **cats are** sleeping.)*

---

The number of a subject is not changed by a phrase following the subject.

    *(The **cats** in the kitchen **are** sleeping.)*

---

The following indefinite pronouns are singular: *anybody, anyone, each, either, everybody, everyone, nobody, neither, no one, one, somebody,* and *someone.*

    *(**Each** of the cats **is** sleeping.)*

---

The following indefinite pronouns are plural: *both, few, many,* and *several.*

    *(**Several** of the cats **are** sleeping.)*

---

The number of the indefinite pronouns *all, any, most, none,* and *some* is determined by the number of the object in the prepositional phrase following the subject. If the pronoun refers to a singular object, the pronoun is singular. If the pronoun refers to a plural object, the pronoun is plural.

    *(**Most** of the **cats are** sleeping. **Most** of their **food is** gone.)*

# SUMMARY OF USES OF THE COMMA

Use commas to separate items in a series

    (1)   If all items in a series are joined by *and* or *or,* do not use commas to separate them.

    (2)   Independent clauses in a series are usually separated by semicolons. Short independent clauses, however, may be separated by commas.

Use commas to separate two or more adjectives preceding a noun.

Use commas before *and, but, or, nor, for, so,* and *yet* when they join independent clauses.

Use commas to set off nonessential clauses and nonessential participial phrases.

Use commas after certain introductory elements.

    (1)   Use a comma after words such as *well, yes, no,* and *why* when they begin a sentence.

    (2)   Use a comma after an introductory participle or participial phrase.

    (3)   Use a comma after a series of introductory prepositional phrases.

    (4)   Use a comma after an introductory adverb clause.

Use commas to set off sentence interrupters.

    (1)   Appositives and appositive phrases are usually set off by commas.

    (2)   Words used in direct address are set off by commas.

    (3)   Parenthetical expressions are set off by commas.

Use commas in certain conventional situations.

    (1)   Use a comma to separate items in dates and addresses.

    (2)   Use a comma after the salutation of a friendly letter and after the closing of any letter.

    (3)   Use a comma after a name followed by an abbreviation such as *Jr., Sr.,* and *M.D.*

Do not use unnecessary commas.

# Chapter 1: Parts of Speech Overview, pp. 1–24

## The Noun, pp. 1–2

### EXERCISE A

1. Look at these photographs of my friend James, who is a relative of Victor.

2. Did the two men visit Madagascar, a large island near Africa?

3. Courage and curiosity are two qualities you will find in my friends.

4. Many different countries make up the large continent of Africa.

5. On his journey back to America, Victor sailed on the Princess.

### EXERCISE B

6. In gym class, Coach Ellis led the students through a set of twenty push-ups.

7. After the children tossed snowballs, they built a snowman on the sidewalk.

8. Did Dad change the batteries in the smoke detector that is in the family room?

9. You should read *Homeless Bird* by Gloria Whelan, a winner of the National Book Award.

10. My sister-in-law, a singer in a band, also plays the guitar.

### EXERCISE C

| | |
|---|---|
| 11. collection | 16. staff |
| 12. pack | 17. squad |
| 13. swarm | 18. council |
| 14. family | 19. pod |
| 15. team | 20. Congress |

## The Pronoun A, pp. 3–4

### EXERCISE A

1. Many teens volunteer their time to worthy causes.

2. Lonny volunteers at an animal shelter. He grooms the dogs.

3. Does Alfredo teach songs to the children at his church?

4. At the local hospital, Nina helps the nurses; she does simple chores for them.

5. Search the Internet for ideas. It lists volunteer programs in many cities.

### EXERCISE B

*(Answers may vary.)*

| | |
|---|---|
| 6. her | 9. him |
| 7. it | 10. I |
| 8. your | |

### EXERCISE C

| | |
|---|---|
| 11. REF | 14. REF |
| 12. INT | 15. INT |
| 13. REF | |

## The Pronoun B, pp. 5–6

### EXERCISE A

1. These are my favorite books of all time.

2. Is this a serious tale of grand adventure, or is it just a silly story?

3. You two should really take a look at these!

4. My skateboard rolls as smoothly as those used in professional competitions.

5. Of the entire football season, that was the most suspenseful game!

6. This set of math problems is a lot like those.

7. When will we finish painting that?

8. Of all of these, the third one sounds the most appealing.

9. That is the first time she's ever eaten a kiwi fruit.

10. Think of this as an opportunity to shine!

**11.** INT          **14.** INT
**12.** DEM          **15.** INT
**13.** DEM

**EXERCISE C**
*(Answers may vary.)*

**16.** those          **19.** this
**17.** these          **20.** Whose
**18.** Which

## The Pronoun C, pp. 7–8
**EXERCISE A**

**1.** Chen is reading *Animal Farm,* <u>which</u> is about power and betrayal.

**2.** George Orwell, <u>who</u> wrote this fable, used animals as main characters.

**3.** The plot is about farm animals <u>that</u> chase away their owners!

**4.** Try reading a book by J.R.R. Tolkien, an author <u>whom</u> many readers admire.

**5.** Bilbo Baggins, <u>whom</u> readers meet in *The Hobbit,* is the hero of this story.

**6.** A hobbit is a creature <u>whose</u> life centers on family, food, and a good home.

**7.** In many classrooms, students read books <u>that</u> explore the dark side of human nature.

**8.** Have you read *Lord of the Flies,* <u>which</u> is about human nature?

**9.** A group of boys, <u>whose</u> airplane crashes, must survive on a lonely island.

**10.** What do you think of these boys, <u>who</u> become savage?

**EXERCISE B**

**11.** The pep rally, <u>which</u> began at one o'clock, lasted almost two hours!

**12.** When should we pick up the uniforms <u>that</u> Ms. Baraka ordered?

**13.** Marie, <u>whom</u> the community greatly admires, planted four trees in a local park.

**14.** Try finding a puzzle piece <u>that</u> is shaped like an H.

**15.** Ernesto's brother, <u>who</u> enjoys good conversation, makes it a point to visit us once a day.

**16.** We saw a whooping crane, <u>which</u> is one of the rarest birds in North America!

**17.** That short story, <u>which</u> talks about the love of a grandmother for her grandson, is excellent.

**18.** Is Leroy, <u>whom</u> our customers love, going to get this month's bonus?

**19.** Julia constructed this model volcano from clay <u>that</u> she found in her own backyard.

**20.** The choir's leaders, <u>who</u> are looking for a new sound, have been listening to Caribbean music.

## The Pronoun D, pp. 9–10
**EXERCISE A**

**1.** <u>All</u> of the hotel's staff members were very helpful.

**2.** <u>Most</u> of the activities, in Jack's opinion, would be fun.

**3.** Of <u>everything</u> available to guests, the shuffleboard court was our favorite spot.

**4.** We played softball with <u>anyone</u> who wanted to play.

**5.** Let's meet Jack and the <u>others</u> at the lake behind the hotel.

**6.** <u>Some</u> of the rocks along the shore are quite beautiful.

**7.** We could give <u>somebody</u> the prettiest stones.

8. Wouldn't Aunt Suzy want a <u>few</u> of them?

9. Save <u>something</u> to help you remember that trip!

10. I think we'd gladly take <u>another</u>.

**EXERCISE B**
*(Answers will vary.)*

11. Each
12. both
13. more
14. anybody
15. Most
16. one
17. everything
18. everyone
19. somebody
20. anyone

## The Adjective, pp. 11–12
**EXERCISE A**

1. There is a <u>large</u> family of <u>healthy</u> ducks by the lake.

2. During the <u>hot</u> afternoon, <u>several</u> deer crossed the <u>grassy</u> meadow.

3. Look at the <u>small</u>, <u>brown</u> rabbit near the trees.

4. A <u>gray</u> dove looked for <u>tiny</u> seeds beneath a <u>leafy</u>, <u>green</u> bush.

5. Did you see the <u>beautiful</u> fur on that fox?

**EXERCISE B**

6. <u>Either</u> coach can train the <u>new</u> team.

7. <u>Which</u> <u>long</u> table will seat the <u>hungry</u> students?

8. <u>Those</u> <u>three</u> rosebushes won't bloom for <u>many</u> weeks.

9. <u>Recent</u> graduates helped <u>several</u> teachers purchase those.

10. We realized that <u>neither</u> frog had been making <u>that</u> <u>unusual</u> noise.

**EXERCISE C**

11. PRO
12. ADJ
13. ADJ
14. N
15. ADJ

## The Verb A, pp. 13–14
**EXERCISE A**

1. John Loudon McAdam <u>designed</u> roads without costly rock foundations.

2. The first self-propelled American land vehicle <u>ran</u> under steam power.

3. The Colorado River toad <u>secretes</u> a poison that <u>can paralyze</u> its predators temporarily.

4. During thunderstorms, lightning bolts <u>create</u> gases that eventually <u>fertilize</u> the soil.

5. Alchemists never <u>produced</u> gold from lead, but they <u>invented</u> some tools that chemists <u>use</u> today.

6. <u>Do</u> mice <u>dream</u>?

7. The tube-shaped leaves of some pitcher plants <u>fill</u> with rainwater and <u>trap</u> insects.

8. Suddenly, hundreds of grasshoppers <u>leapt</u> into the air.

9. When a bug <u>is caught</u> in the sticky hairs of a sundew's leaf, the leaf <u>curls</u> around it.

10. On the longest day of summer in the Antarctic Circle, the sun never <u>sets</u>.

**EXERCISE B**

11. INT
12. TR
13. TR
14. INT
15. INT
16. INT
17. INT
18. TR
19. TR
20. INT

## The Verb B, pp. 15–16
**EXERCISE A**

1. Cassie thought that the radishes <u>tasted</u> wonderful.

2. Sandals <u>are</u> usually a good, comfortable shoe for warm weather.

3. <u>Is</u> Janelle's poster the one with the piano full of flowers on it?

4. The cricket in my room <u>seemed</u> noisy last night.

5. Mel <u>looks</u> confident; maybe she <u>should be</u> in charge.

6. This paint job <u>could have been</u> perfect, but the paint dripped.

7. Sophia <u>became</u> the first of us to ask, "<u>Were</u> cars really that slow back then?"

8. That mockingbird certainly <u>sounds</u> carefree.

9. His grandmother <u>was</u> one of the first women to teach at a university.

10. The music <u>stayed</u> loud and festive, even when the band <u>grew</u> tired.

**EXERCISE B**

__L__ 11. Over the years, the (lock) <u>had become</u> (rusty).

__A__ 12. With great difficulty, Lisa <u>turned</u> the key in the lock.

__L__ 13. Inside, the empty (house) <u>seemed</u> perfectly (silent).

__L__ 14. Long ago, the dusty (air) <u>had turned</u> (stale).

__L__ 15. (Lisa) <u>remained</u> (calm) in spite of the eerie atmosphere.

__L__ 16. Then (she) stood on the porch and <u>felt</u> (better).

__A__ 17. She <u>could smell</u> fresh-cut hay in the breeze.

__A__ 18. Crops <u>grew</u> in the fields across the street from the house.

__L__ 19. With a new coat of paint, (it) <u>might be</u> a nice (place) to live.

__L__ 20. The (house) suddenly <u>appeared</u> far less (spooky).

**The Verb C, pp. 17–18**
**EXERCISE A**

1. Pumpkins <u>are known</u> for their soft orange pulp and high water content.

2. You <u>may have eaten</u> delicious pumpkin bread or pumpkin muffins.

3. That pumpkin <u>was grown</u> in Margaret's own backyard garden.

4. It <u>had become</u> ripe for harvest a few days ago.

5. The tough orange rind <u>must be removed</u> from the pumpkin.

6. Then, the orange pulp <u>can be used</u> for food.

7. We <u>can save</u> some of the seeds for next year's crop.

8. <u>Should</u> we <u>toast</u> the rest of the pumpkinseeds?

9. During late October, many people <u>will carve</u> a pumpkin.

10. Pumpkins <u>have</u> also <u>been grown</u> as food for livestock.

**EXERCISE B**

11. <u>Do</u> you <u>enjoy</u> ice-skating and other winter sports?

12. Diego and I <u>have</u> often <u>watched</u> skating competitions on television.

13. I myself <u>have</u> never <u>worn</u> a pair of ice skates.

14. My sister, however, <u>will</u> frequently <u>compete</u> in skating matches.

15. The coldness of the icy arena <u>doesn't bother</u> her.

16. Since childhood, she <u>has</u> always <u>enjoyed</u> the competitive nature of sports.

17. You <u>should</u> not <u>have missed</u> the competition last week.

18. Will you <u>attend</u> the match on Saturday afternoon?

19. We <u>have</u> always <u>sat</u> in one of the front rows.

20. We <u>will</u> not <u>miss</u> a single bit of action from those great seats.

## The Adverb, pp. 19–20

**EXERCISE A**

1. Please write your new phone number <u>there</u>.

2. <u>Loudly</u>, the telephone in Becca's room rang.

3. <u>Where</u> did she earn the money for her own phone?

4. Becca mows lawns <u>weekly</u> for extra money.

5. She had <u>carefully</u> saved money for the phone.

**EXERCISE B**

6. Whose <u>incredibly</u> delicious casserole is this?

7. <u>Rather</u> large trees surround the car lot.

8. After a long afternoon, I can say my chores are <u>nearly</u> complete.

9. An <u>especially</u> valuable player receives the MVP award.

10. Please give a snack to the children, who are <u>slightly</u> hungry.

**EXERCISE C**

11. Why is he speaking <u>very</u> quietly?

12. <u>Somewhat</u> excitedly, the child accepted the gift.

13. Both students completed the test <u>equally</u> quickly.

14. A fire broke out, but firefighters arrived <u>quite</u> soon.

15. You interpreted the poem <u>extremely</u> creatively.

## The Preposition, pp. 21–22

**EXERCISE A**

1. Everyone was frightened <u>during</u> the scary <u>movie</u>.

2. <u>Without</u> a <u>hat</u>, Ellen's hair always lightens.

3. Jeff, you can use chicken <u>in place of</u> the <u>beef</u>.

4. The beautiful full moon disappeared <u>behind</u> thick <u>clouds</u>.

5. How can I choose <u>between</u> two good <u>choices</u>?

**EXERCISE B**

6. Because of the <u>fire</u>, smoke billowed <u>from</u> the <u>windows</u> and <u>doors</u>.

7. <u>Since</u> last <u>Monday</u>, I have been leaving the house <u>before</u> <u>you</u> each morning.

8. The story is <u>about</u> a <u>horse</u> that gallops <u>next to</u> <u>bicyclists</u>.

9. <u>Aside from</u> a few loose <u>boards</u>, the bridge <u>across</u> the <u>stream</u> looks safe.

10. Look <u>at</u> the perfect <u>blanket</u> <u>of</u> <u>snow</u> <u>on</u> the <u>streets</u> and <u>lawns</u>.

11. Felicia skipped <u>through</u> the open <u>gate</u> <u>in front of</u> her <u>house</u>.

12. <u>In addition to</u> old <u>newspapers</u>, Toni collects cans <u>during</u> recycling <u>drives</u>.

13. Couldn't we use the tomatoes we grew <u>instead of</u> <u>those</u> <u>from</u> a <u>store</u>?

14. Since he got to sit <u>behind</u> the <u>dugout</u>, Cedric stayed <u>through</u> the final <u>inning</u>.

15. Should we climb <u>aboard</u> the <u>boat</u> <u>beside</u> the <u>dock</u>?

## The Conjunction and the Interjection, pp. 23–24

**EXERCISE A**

1. I had met the girl before, <u>yet</u> I couldn't remember her name.

2. We heard the fire alarm <u>not only</u> in the hallways <u>but also</u> in the classrooms.

3. After the assembly, I couldn't find Mark <u>or</u> Chi anywhere.

4. Do you know <u>whether</u> Carlos sanded <u>or</u> painted the bookcase?

5. On the beach <u>and</u> in the water, the family played happily.

6. Mr. Paulson had expected <u>neither</u> the award <u>nor</u> the party.

7. Was <u>either</u> the principal <u>or</u> the vice-principal present at the ceremony?

8. I will enjoy the winter break, <u>but</u> I will miss my friends.

9. Will this bus take us to <u>both</u> the mall <u>and</u> the library?

10. <u>Neither</u> the computer <u>nor</u> the printer was turned on.

**EXERCISE B**

| | |
|---|---|
| **11.** CRD | **16.** INT |
| **12.** INT | **17.** CORR |
| **13.** CORR | **18.** INT |
| **14.** CRD | **19.** CRD |
| **15.** INT | **20.** CORR |

## Chapter 2: The Parts of a Sentence, pp. 25–38

### The Subject, pp. 25–26

**EXERCISE A**

1. The light above the sink went out yesterday.

2. The biology students collected different types of leaves.

3. Did Dad enjoy the baseball game?

4. The purple and blue flowers really brightened up the room.

5. When will the band members return from the field trip?

**EXERCISE B**

6. The great pyramids of Egypt have become famous.

7. They were used as royal burial chambers.

8. Have you ever seen a pyramid?

9. Many different cultures built pyramids.

10. Examples of these unique structures can be found in Egypt and Mexico.

**EXERCISE C**

11. Turtles and bullfrogs lived at the edge of the lake.

12. Neither onions nor peppers were in the stew.

13. Did Rosa, Barbara, and Fredric work together on the experiment?

14. Not only the cows but also the chickens must be fed.

15. Sally or Eugene will give a speech today.

### The Predicate, pp. 27–28

**EXERCISE A**

1. drank

2. will practice

3. should show

4. shone

5. must have found

**EXERCISE B**

6. The basketball team will be playing in the semifinals.

7. Does your aunt own the nursery on Park Street?

8. In the shade of the oak tree, grass does not grow.

9. Calvin has been taking piano lessons for five years.

10. The kittens are playing.

**EXERCISE C**

11. Both tennis players inspected their rackets and practiced their swings.

12. Would you run the cash register or wrap purchases for me?

13. The bird had collected bits of straw and made a nest.

14. High above the crowd, the trapeze artists swung and leaped gracefully.

15. In the afternoon, my dogs sit on the patio and wait for me.

### Predicate Nominatives, pp. 29–30

**EXERCISE A**

1. goldfish

2. Mr. Nelson

3. teacher

4. these

5. farmer

**EXERCISE B**

6. city hall

7. instructor

8. architect

9. William Carlos Williams

10. she

11. volunteers

12. member

13. friend

14. fund-raisers

15. bluebonnets

16. Sally Chavez, Fred Browning

17. accountant, coach

18. judge

19. pants, sweater

20. sea horse

21. aunt, uncle, cousins

22. jewels, coins

23. Ms. Ferguson, Mr. Price, Mrs. Martinez

24. contestant, judge

25. she

## Predicate Adjectives, pp. 31–32

### EXERCISE A

1. muddy

2. beautiful

3. salty

4. clean

5. friendly

6. interesting

7. creative

8. exhausted

9. organized

10. gloomy

### EXERCISE B

11. interesting, suspenseful

12. enjoyable, boring

13. fantastic

14. happy

15. modern, speedy, reliable

16. sweet

17. shy, friendly

18. thirsty

19. long

20. energetic, playful, entertaining

## Direct Objects, pp. 33–34

### EXERCISE A

1. Abraham Lincoln

2. scores

3. acorns

4. cashier

5. *The Wizard of Oz*

6. rabbit

7. bikes

8. Michelle

9. cans

10. village

### EXERCISE B

11. glue, tape

12. smile

13. Clara Ruiz, Kate Samson

14. novels, short stories, plays, essays, poems

15. me

16. pots, pans

17. crowd

18. scarf, jacket

19. bin, can

20. claws

## Indirect Objects, pp. 35–36

### EXERCISE A

1. Debbie

2. everyone

3. me

4. Karen

5. children

6. me

7. her

8. Maurice

9. you

10. Sasha

### EXERCISE B

11. Spotty, Skeeter

12. you, sister

13. Marla, Nancy

14. Isabel, Alex

15. student, teacher

16. Lee, Fred

17. Jill, me

18. Carrie, Leo

19. brother, me

20. teacher, principal

## Classifying Sentences by Purpose, pp. 37–38

**EXERCISE A**

| | |
|---|---|
| 1. DEC | 6. IMP |
| 2. IMP | 7. DEC |
| 3. IMP | 8. IMP |
| 4. DEC | 9. IMP |
| 5. DEC | 10. DEC |

**EXERCISE B**

INT    **11.** . . . campaign?

IMP    **12.** . . . edge!

EXC    **13.** . . . test! [or

DEC    . . . test.]

DEC    **14.** . . . sweater.

IMP    **15.** . . . theater.

INT    **16.** . . . swing?

EXC    **17.** . . . have!

DEC    **18.** . . . friends.

INT    **19.** . . . tomorrow?

IMP    **20.** . . . out!

# Chapter 3: The Phrase, pp. 39–50

## The Prepositional Phrase A, pp. 39–40

**EXERCISE A**

**1.** Can you read the name <u>on the blue boat</u>?

**2.** Early <u>in the morning</u>, Earl fishes <u>for shrimp</u>.

**3.** Often, he also looks <u>for crabs and lobsters</u>.

**4.** The storm <u>at sea</u> probably will not come <u>near our coastal town</u>.

**5.** Look <u>at the beautiful sailboat</u> <u>in the harbor</u>!

**EXERCISE B**

**6.** Students <u>throughout the school</u> are happy it snowed today.

**7.** Did your lab partner take notes <u>about the experiment's results</u>?

**8.** Someone left the door <u>to the garage</u> open.

**9.** Is that my notebook <u>near the lunch tray</u> <u>on the table</u>?

**10.** The poster <u>near the water fountain</u> <u>outside our classroom</u> looks ancient.

**11.** Some people <u>from our neighborhood</u> are painting the sign <u>next to the entrance</u>.

**12.** Let's take the gravel path <u>around the observatory</u>.

**13.** Stories <u>about the cost</u> <u>of a new bicycle frame</u> are all too true!

**14.** The kingfishers <u>along the river</u> always chatter when they fly.

**15.** The fans grew quiet once they heard the buzzer <u>before the game</u>.

## The Prepositional Phrase B, pp. 41–42

**EXERCISE A**

**1.** <u>Because of rust</u>, the gate in the stone wall would not open.

**2.** Darcy has always been great <u>at shortstop</u>.

**3.** <u>During the morning</u>, the horses walked <u>in Central Park</u>.

**4.** <u>Before the game</u>, do the cheerleaders practice their cheers?

**5.** You can stay <u>for a few days</u> <u>in our apartment</u>.

**6.** Allergies have left Paulette's voice hoarse <u>beyond description</u>.

**7.** We followed the fossil dinosaur tracks <u>into the streambed</u>.

**8.** The loudest of the seven frogs lives <u>among those reeds</u>.

**9.** This clip, <u>according to the manual</u>, should connect the spring <u>to the hood</u>.

**10.** Just drag the nylon line <u>across the creek's surface</u>.

**EXERCISE B**

**11.** Yolanda is wonderful <u>in the play's leading role</u>.

**12.** We left <u>for the museum</u> <u>at nine o'clock</u>.

**13.** Were the costumes finished <u>in time</u> <u>for the fair</u>? [or Were the costumes finished <u>in time for the fair</u>?]

**14.** <u>On spring afternoons</u>, thunderstorms form <u>throughout this region</u>.

**15.** This glass is slick <u>across its surface</u>.

**16.** Skilled <u>with computers</u>, Daisy wrote a program that generates model atoms.

**17.** This net should be large enough <u>for several hundred prom-night balloons</u>.

**18.** <u>On our trip</u>, we journeyed <u>past a huge statue</u> of Paul Bunyan.

**19.** This fireplace, <u>before the first big cold snap</u>, seemed uncalled-for.

**20.** Melanie felt enthusiastic <u>about her sister's medical research</u>.

## The Participle and the Participial Phrase, pp. 43–44

### EXERCISE A

1. Ada's <u>exhausted</u> teammates sat together on the bench.

2. Her <u>hushed</u> friends watched Ada step to the plate.

3. Suddenly, a <u>speeding</u> runner stole third base.

4. The pitcher threw a <u>wavering</u> curveball right down the middle.

5. Ada hit it solidly and drove in the <u>winning</u> run.

### EXERCISE B

6. The bus stopped next to a building <u>surrounded by statues.</u>

7. <u>Re-reading my essay,</u> I discovered that two words were missing.

8. The light <u>cast by the aquarium's fluorescent bulb</u> was bright.

9. During the recital, several parents chuckled at their <u>wildly dancing</u> toddlers.

10. <u>Baked with cinnamon,</u> the apples were delicious.

11. How many birds <u>living in this open field</u> have you identified?

12. <u>Opening the blinds,</u> Ms. Saadi faced the <u>newly risen</u> sun.

13. The cowboy's story, <u>sprinkled with wit,</u> kept his audience laughing.

14. <u>Snuffling noisily together,</u> the hounds explored an old shoe.

15. How long do <u>closely guarded</u> secrets really stay secret?

## The Gerund and the Gerund Phrase, pp. 45–46

### EXERCISE A

1. dunking
2. mewing, meowing
3. Catching
4. practicing
5. singing

### EXERCISE B

6. The choir gave <u>preparing for the concert</u> their full attention.

7. <u>Slowly and carefully detailing his car</u> is Kim's favorite task.

8. Would you help me with <u>hanging these posters?</u>

9. The ball's <u>bouncing into the stands</u> surprised everyone.

10. The firefighter's heroic act was <u>daringly rescuing an entire family.</u>

11. Clara's latest amusement is <u>cheaply collecting memorabilia from the seventies.</u>

12. We practiced <u>quickly passing the ball to our forwards.</u>

13. <u>Boiling gently in water</u> will cook the pasta.

14. Who hasn't enjoyed <u>heartily laughing at one comedian or another?</u>

15. <u>A distant clattering along the rails</u> was the first sign of the subway car's approach.

## The Infinitive and the Infinitive Phrase, pp. 47–48

### EXERCISE A

1. One book <u>to read</u> is *Cranford* by Elizabeth Gaskell.

2. After I'd laced up my high-tops, I was eager <u>to play.</u>

3. Is a foreign language easy <u>to learn?</u>

4. Ready to run, members of the track team lined up at their marks.

5. To cook is not a simple task.

**EXERCISE B**

6. To make his wheelchair go forward, Chris presses on this lever.

7. At the playoffs, her dream to photograph sports stars was fulfilled.

8. Your next responsibility is to make good grades in school.

9. To entertain was the juggler's goal for each performance.

10. The pill bug has the ability to roll itself into a tiny ball.

11. Stock these shelves carefully to keep the soup cans from falling.

12. Was this software designed to create new Web pages?

13. David and Alma want to try out for roles in *Our Town.*

14. Either red pepper or curry powder is a suitable spice to use in that recipe.

15. We need to carry these boxes of files to the office.

**The Appositive and the Appositive Phrase, pp. 49–50**

**EXERCISE A**

1. My home state, Oregon, is on the West Coast.

2. The country Japan is an island in the Pacific Ocean.

3. Have you ever seen photographs of her, Justice Sandra Day O'Connor?

4. Deliver this gift, a houseplant, to our new neighbors.

5. The athlete Carl Lewis won nine Olympic gold medals in track and field.

6. Glimpses of his own past helped transform the penny-pincher Scrooge into a new person.

7. Connect this belt to the part of the alternator that fits it, the pulley.

8. The engineers Gottlieb Daimler and Wilhelm Maybach built a motorized bicycle in 1885.

9. Safely landing the lunar module *Eagle,* Neil Armstrong and Edwin E. Aldrin, Jr. became the first people to walk on the moon.

10. During the Roaring Twenties, the Jazz Age, many Americans ignored distress in Europe.

**EXERCISE B**

11. Volcanoes, the subject of my report, are vents in the earth's crust.

12. Use one of those, the lockers in the bottom row, for your gym clothes.

13. Did all of them enjoy the main dish, a mix of vegetables and pasta?

14. Find the brightest planet, the hot-surfaced Venus, in the night sky.

15. A small, five-armed creature with a spiny skeleton, a starfish, washed ashore.

16. The busy highway the Lincoln Turnpike is undergoing repairs this week.

17. Robert Browning wrote *The Ring and the Book,* the tale of a Roman trial.

18. My friends and I like salsa, a fast and energetic kind of dance music.

19. Did you hear that, a loud buzzing outside the window?

20. Captain of the team, Mel decided the batters' lineup.

# Chapter 4: The Clause, pp. 51–60

## The Adjective Clause, pp. 51–52

### EXERCISE A

1. The <u>people</u> <u>who read that book</u> didn't like the story's ending.

2. I spoke to <u>Aaron</u>, <u>whose locker is near mine</u>, after study hall.

3. Have you seen the action <u>movie that opened on Friday</u>?

4. The <u>spot</u> <u>where we build the campfire</u> should be in an open area.

5. Meet <u>Anya</u>, <u>whom you will tutor for English class</u>.

### EXERCISE B

6. Carver was born in a time <u>when slavery was still practiced</u>.

7. Is the war <u>that ended legal slavery in the United States</u> the Civil War?

8. In his late twenties, Carver, <u>who had held a variety of odd jobs</u>, graduated from high school.

9. His artistic skills surfaced during his childhood, <u>which he spent on a plantation</u>.

10. As a boy Carver learned to draw, and as he grew older, he painted pictures of the plants <u>that grew around him</u>.

11. Carver, <u>whose college degree was in agricultural science</u>, first studied art and piano.

12. Is Carver a scholar <u>whom you would imitate</u>?

13. The <u>place</u> <u>where he earned his bachelor's degree</u> was Iowa State Agricultural College.

14. Tell me about the master of science degree <u>that he earned in 1896</u>.

15. He donated his <u>life savings</u> to the Carver Research Foundation, <u>which he helped establish</u>.

## The Adverb Clause, pp. 53–54

### EXERCISE A

1. <u>As she dances</u>, Kimi moves <u>gracefully</u>.

2. <u>If you have already read this book</u>, do not <u>tell</u> me the conclusion.

3. Coach has made volleyball practice sessions <u>longer</u> <u>so that we'll get better</u>.

4. Derek <u>plays</u> songs on the guitar <u>whenever he is feeling cheerful</u>.

5. <u>Since you know French</u>, <u>will</u> you <u>translate</u> this for me?

### EXERCISE B

6. <u>Before Sue took her palomino to the horse show</u>, she groomed the horse carefully.

7. Was the golden retriever friendlier <u>than the Great Dane was</u>?

8. <u>If the weather is cold</u>, we will exercise inside the gym.

9. The brothers usually behave <u>as if they are best friends</u>.

10. Shannon painted slowly <u>so that the brush strokes were distinct</u>.

## The Noun Clause, pp. 55–56

### EXERCISE A

1. Does <u>what the parrot says</u> make you laugh?

2. The scientist's only concern was <u>whether the experiment was a success</u>.

3. <u>That the plan worked</u> surprised us both.

4. The trouble with the engine is <u>what I expected</u>.

5. <u>Whoever chooses to report on this book</u> will get an extra week to finish reading it.

6. According to Beth, quick and accurate revision is <u>why she uses a computer</u>.

7. <u>Whatever venture Rosa supports</u> becomes successful.

8. Is <u>whoever moved the queen's crown</u> still in the palace?

9. The show's finest moments were <u>when the magician pretended to read minds</u>.

10. "<u>Where the trail ends</u>" is our club's new slogan.

**EXERCISE B**

11. After an hour's hike, we found <u>where the others had made camp</u>.

12. Nathan gave <u>whatever was dirty</u> a thorough scrub.

13. In her writer's journal, she records <u>whatever happens to her each day</u>.

14. Michael gave <u>whether to enter the contest</u> some serious thought.

15. According to the ranger, a bear will eat <u>whatever it feels like eating</u>.

16. <u>Whoever returned her wallet</u> deserves her thanks.

17. Set those potted plants near <u>where the children dug the holes</u>.

18. Ms. Ortega suddenly realized <u>why the pack seemed heavy</u>.

19. Do you sometimes send funny e-mails to <u>whomever you know</u>?

20. Give <u>whichever hedge is too tall</u> a trim.

## Sentence Structure A, pp. 57–58
**EXERCISE A**

___S___ 1. <u>Several brushes were inside the barn</u>.

___N___ 2. <u>Nicole brushed her horse Rowdy's mane</u>, and <u>then she cleaned his hooves</u>, <u>which were muddy</u>.

___N___ 3. <u>Is that a new saddle</u>, or <u>is it one of the older ones</u>?

___S___ 4. In the pasture, <u>a horse and her foal grazed quietly and watched Rowdy</u>.

___N___ 5. Nearby, <u>as Nicole brushed her horse</u>, <u>a barn cat and her kittens played</u>.

**EXERCISE B**

| | | | |
|---|---|---|---|
| 6. S | | 11. CD | |
| 7. CD | | 12. CD | |
| 8. S | | 13. CD | |
| 9. S | | 14. S | |
| 10. S | | 15. CD | |

## Sentence Structure B, pp. 59–60
**EXERCISE A**

___CX___ 1. <u>Since he can't fix the leak</u>, <u>Alan will call a plumber</u>.

___N___ 2. <u>Do you have the phone number for a reliable plumber</u>?

___CX___ 3. <u>On Thursday afternoon, he'll leave work early</u> <u>so that he can meet the plumber</u>.

___CX___ 4. <u>After the leak is fixed</u>, <u>he'll mop up the water</u> <u>because guests are coming</u>.

___N___ 5. <u>Tina and Anthony will arrive on Thursday and will stay for the weekend</u>.

**EXERCISE B**

_CD-CX_ **6.** Until metal pens were made in the mid-nineteenth century, people wrote with brushes or reeds, or they used quill pens.

_CX_ **7.** After metal pens and pen tips came into use, quill pens fell out of use.

_CX_ **8.** Have you heard of John Mitchell, who invented a machine-made steel pen tip in 1828?

_CD-CX_ **9.** Because a person continually dipped the pen into an ink supply, these pens could be messy; therefore, inventors looked for a better design.

_CD-CX_ **10.** In 1884, L. E. Waterman produced the fountain pen, which held the ink supply within the pen, and the design became popular.

_CX_ **11.** The new ballpoint pen was released before the century ended.

_CD-CX_ **12.** Some people wrote with ballpoint pens in 1895, yet Lazlo Biro designed a better model that was used worldwide by the mid-1940s.

_CX_ **13.** The "biro" is similar to the older fountain pen that held a reservoir of ink.

_CD-CX_ **14.** The ballpoint pen holds ink in its reservoir; because a metal ball at its tip rotates, the tip becomes coated in ink.

_CX_ **15.** Did you know that soft-tip pens came into use during the 1960s?

_Developmental Language Skills Answer Key_     **15**

# Chapter 5: Agreement, pp. 61–68

## Subject-Verb Agreement A, pp. 61–62

### EXERCISE A
1. brings
2. remind
3. enjoy
4. drink
5. Does

### EXERCISE B
6. Have
7. look
8. bring
9. talk
10. are

### EXERCISE C
11. expect
12. Do
13. is
14. needs
15. protect

## Subject-Verb Agreement B, pp. 63–64

### EXERCISE A
1. is
2. brings
3. turns
4. plans
5. Does

### EXERCISE B
6. have
7. were
8. are
9. Are
10. compete

### EXERCISE C
11. have
12. Is
13. refuse
14. are
15. Does

## Pronoun-Antecedent Agreement A, pp. 65–66

### EXERCISE A
1. his
2. they
3. its
4. her
5. their

### EXERCISE B
6. their
7. his
8. their
9. them
10. it
11. her
12. their
13. her
14. their
15. his

## Pronoun-Antecedent Agreement B, pp. 67–68

### EXERCISE A
1. its
2. his or her
3. its
4. her
5. his or her

### EXERCISE B
6. their
7. themselves
8. their
9. their
10. they

### EXERCISE C
11. their
12. them
13. It
14. their
15. it

## Chapter 6: Using Verbs Correctly, pp. 69–82

### Principal Parts of Verbs A, pp. 69–70

**EXERCISE A**

1. elect _____elected_____ [have] _____elected_____
2. clean _____cleaned_____ [have] _____cleaned_____
3. provide _____provided_____ [have] _____provided_____
4. play _____played_____ [have] _____played_____
5. gain _____gained_____ [have] _____gained_____

**EXERCISE B**

6. grab _____grabbed_____ [have] _____grabbed_____
7. suppose _____supposed_____ [have] _____supposed_____
8. drown _____drowned_____ [have] _____drowned_____
9. prejudice _____prejudiced_____ [have] _____prejudiced_____
10. use _____used_____ [have] _____used_____

**EXERCISE C**

11. pushed
12. practicing
13. mentioned
14. planted
15. picked

### Principal Parts of Verbs B, pp. 71–72

**EXERCISE A**

1. burst
2. set
3. let
4. hit
5. cost

**EXERCISE B**

6. spent
7. heard
8. made
9. built
10. bent

**EXERCISE C**

11. ran
12. stung
13. slid
14. drank
15. won

**EXERCISE D**

16. sought
17. gone
18. grown
19. tore
20. written

### Tense, pp. 73–74

**EXERCISE A**

1. future
2. present
3. past
4. past
5. future

**EXERCISE B**

6. present perfect
7. present perfect
8. past perfect
9. past perfect
10. future perfect

**EXERCISE C**

11. wrote
12. had bought
13. has thought
14. will finish
15. have learned

### Progressive Forms, pp. 75–76

**EXERCISE A**

1. future progressive
2. past progressive
3. present progressive
4. past progressive
5. present progressive

**EXERCISE B**

6. present perfect progressive
7. past perfect progressive
8. present perfect progressive
9. future perfect progressive
10. past perfect progressive

## EXERCISE C

**11.** had sent

**12.** will have heard

**13.** have written

**14.** have been telling

**15.** said

## Consistency of Tense, pp. 77–78

### EXERCISE A

| | | | |
|---|---|---|---|
| **1.** I | | **6.** I | |
| **2.** C | | **7.** C | |
| **3.** I | | **8.** C | |
| **4.** I | | **9.** I | |
| **5.** C | | **10.** I | |

### EXERCISE B

*Answers may vary slightly.*

**11.** The haze cleared away, and the day was beautiful. [*or* The haze will clear away, and the day will be beautiful.]

**12.** The student council will vote and will choose a location for the class picnic. [*or* The student council voted and chose a location for the class picnic.]

**13.** A pair of kingfishers hunt for fish while we watch. [*or* A pair of kingfishers hunted for fish while we watched.]

**14.** The wind blew through the trees, and leaves fell to the ground. [*or* The wind blows through the trees, and leaves fall to the ground.]

**15.** When will the computer store hold its grand opening and allow customers to come in?

## Active and Passive Voice, pp. 79–80

### EXERCISE A

| | | | |
|---|---|---|---|
| **1.** AV | | **6.** PV | |
| **2.** PV | | **7.** AV | |
| **3.** AV | | **8.** AV | |
| **4.** PV | | **9.** AV | |
| **5.** AV | | **10.** PV | |

## EXERCISE B

**11.** The receiver caught the ball.

**12.** Mom and Dad painted the walls.

**13.** Will you answer the phone?

**14.** C, The performer of the action is unknown.

**15.** My big sister caught a cold.

## *Lie* and *Lay, Sit* and *Set, Rise* and *Raise,* pp. 81–82

### EXERCISE A

**1.** laid

**2.** lie

**3.** lay

**4.** laid

**5.** lay

### EXERCISE B

**6.** set

**7.** sitting

**8.** sat

**9.** set

**10.** Sitting

### EXERCISE C

**11.** raise

**12.** rising

**13.** rose

**14.** risen

**15.** rise

# Chapter 7: Using Pronouns Correctly, pp. 83–92

## The Nominative Case, pp. 83–84

### EXERCISE A
1. they
2. he
3. They
4. We
5. she

### EXERCISE B
6. he
7. she
8. I
9. they
10. he

### EXERCISE C
11. we
12. I
13. he
14. they
15. she

## The Objective Case, pp. 85–86

### EXERCISE A
1. us
2. her
3. them
4. us
5. me

### EXERCISE B
6. me
7. us
8. him
9. them
10. her

### EXERCISE C
11. me
12. them
13. him and her
14. them
15. him and me

## Special Problems in Pronoun Usage, pp. 87–88

### EXERCISE A
1. whom
2. Who
3. whoever
4. Who
5. whom
6. who
7. whom
8. who
9. whom
10. whomever

### EXERCISE B
11. we
12. her
13. us
14. We
15. her

## Clear Reference A, pp. 89–90

### EXERCISE A
*The arrows are to help students determine whether the reference is clear or ambiguous. They are not meant to be graded, though the teacher may require them.*

__C__ 1. After the boys talked to the coach, <u>he</u> advised them to run some wind sprints.

__A__ 2. My uncle asked his son to bring <u>his</u> snow boots <u>inside</u>.

__A__ 3. Zach let Brian know that <u>his</u> backpack was out in the hall.

__A__ 4. Have the girls taken the puppies to <u>their</u> home yet?

__C__ 5. Make sure that Carrie knows <u>her</u> lines and that Jason has his costume ready.

__A__ 6. The ship rolled on the wave as <u>it</u> ran across the ocean.

___C___ **7.** After Sonia finished her solo, the crowd cheered.

___A___ **8.** Margaret e-mailed her aunt about her recipe for pasta salad.

___A___ **9.** Did the artists or the viewers say that they enjoyed the exhibit?

___C___ **10.** Is Mars the brightest planet this month, or is it Venus?

**EXERCISE B**

*Answers will vary slightly, but references should be clear.*

**11.** After Billy and José left band practice, Billy realized he'd left his notebook behind.

**12.** I enjoyed watching the helicopter as it created a small dust cloud.

**13.** While Doug and Terrell were at the airport, Terrell ran into a friend from elementary school.

**14.** The day after she bought the blue skirt and the yellow dress, Tisha wore the dress to school.

**15.** As Mr. Moreno and Mrs. Burke presented an award to the soccer team, the players had smiles on their faces.

## Clear Reference B, pp. 91–92

**EXERCISE A**

**1.** C

**2.** G

**3.** G

**4.** G

**5.** C

**EXERCISE B**

*Answers will vary, but references should be clear.*

**6.** Myra is proud of her mother, not only for finishing school, but also for becoming a firefighter.

**7.** The volunteers found that the hard work of raking leaves and putting up a fence was rewarding.

**8.** Being around our neighbor's animals usually makes me sneeze—she has two cats and three birds.

**9.** Waves splashed the dock, and a cold wind blew. The storm caused everyone to rush inside.

**10.** The uneventful drive from Austin to Dallas took the family three hours.

## Chapter 8: Using Modifiers Correctly, pp. 93–98

### Comparison of Modifiers, pp. 93–94

**EXERCISE A**

1. more exciting
2. clearest
3. greener [*or* more green]
4. easier
5. least elastic
6. most likely
7. most trustworthy
8. more helpful
9. less purple
10. fewer

**EXERCISE B**

11. scarier
12. most aggressive
13. more challenging
14. hardest
15. more difficult

### Placement of Modifiers A, pp. 95–96

**EXERCISE A**

1. D
2. C
3. D
4. D
5. C
6. C
7. D
8. C
9. D
10. C

**EXERCISE B**

*(Answers will vary.)*

11. Exhausted and thirsty, the team thought that the locker room looked welcoming.
12. The first stars of the evening, shimmering faintly, appeared as we watched.
13. As Jan disconnected the car's battery, the horn began to blow.

14. To successfully perform this experiment, you will need hours of preparation.
15. Picking up the phone, Tony heard his mom's voice loud and clear.

### Placement of Modifiers B, pp. 97–98

**EXERCISE A**

1. M
2. C
3. M
4. M
5. C

**EXERCISE B**

6. The painting covered the wall <u>in its heavy gold frame</u>.
7. It's time to put the tools into the tool chest <u>you were using to fix the car</u>.
8. <u>Rocking in her lap</u>, Grandmother soothed her grandson.
9. <u>Freshly picked from the tree</u>, breakfast consisted of delicious peaches.
10. The flag was flapping in the wind, <u>wrapping itself around the pole</u>.

**EXERCISE C**

*(Answers will vary.)*

11. Janice regarded her garden, withered in the sun, with dismay.
12. Please bring me the book that has no back cover from the shelf.
13. The geologist tapped lightly on the crystals embedded in the rock.
14. The sun set with a fiery glow as we watched.
15. The mouse, which wanted to hide from the hawk, skittered into the woodpile.

# Chapter 9: A Glossary of Usage, pp. 99–104

## A Glossary of Usage A, pp. 99–100

### EXERCISE A

1. An
2. accept
3. I'm not
4. except
5. an
6. a
7. accepted
8. aren't
9. an
10. excepted

### EXERCISE B

11. books
12. among
13. a lot
14. between
15. a lot
16. are
17. between
18. a lot
19. among
20. be

## A Glossary of Usage B, pp. 101–102

### EXERCISE A

1. fewer
2. take
3. must have
4. bring
5. less
6. Take
7. less
8. should have
9. fewer
10. must have

### EXERCISE B

11. its
12. well
13. themselves
14. rather
15. It's
16. himself
17. its
18. rather
19. good
20. It's

## A Glossary of Usage C, pp. 103–104

### EXERCISE A

1. There
2. Those
3. their
4. then
5. their

### EXERCISE B

6. your
7. try to
8. You're
9. your
10. try to

### EXERCISE C

11. any
12. can
13. anything
14. Have
15. any

## Chapter 10: Capital Letters, pp. 105–18
### Capitalization A, pp. 105–106
#### EXERCISE A

1. I think she said, "(P)lease take your shoes out of the kitchen."

2. "(W)ho has my pencil?" asked Maria.

3. Daniel smiled and said, "(B)oy, this movie's ending sure surprised me."

4. (S)ome of the most well-known features of that national park are its glaciers.

5. Her eyes grew wide and she whispered, "(D)id you hear that?"

6. (H)e says that he's going to try out for our soccer team this year.

7. (I)t'll be wonderful to add a trophy or two to the cases in the front hallway.

8. My father nodded and said, "(T)he metal frame of this dock was made to last."

9. (A)s long as we're standing here, keep your chin up and your shoulders back.

10. (H)ow many blades are on the propeller of that helicopter?

#### EXERCISE B
11. (M)y dearest Miss Bennet,

12. (Y)ours faithfully,

13. (D)ear Service Manager:

14. (S)incerely yours,

15. (D)ear Mom and Dad,

#### EXERCISE C
16. In every one of my photographs, (I) look sleepy.

17. "We are going to pick up the package," (I) told them.

18. Maybe (I)'m in the mood for a long stroll.

19. "Perhaps," Chi laughed, "he and (I) should rewrite the letter."

20. You would think that (I)'d never eaten spaghetti before.

### Capitalization B, pp. 107–108
#### EXERCISE A
1. **b.** Madison Avenue
2. **b.** month
3. **b.** Carver Middle School
4. **a.** Wednesday
5. **a.** San Antonio Spurs
6. **b.** Queen Victoria
7. **a.** hero
8. **b.** Idaho
9. **a.** those limestone caves
10. **a.** Boston

#### EXERCISE B
*Answers will vary. Sample responses are provided.*

11. The funniest <u>person</u> I have ever met is named <u>Sheila Singleton</u>.

12. She named her <u>horse</u> <u>Red Chief</u>.

13. The <u>coach</u> says that his middle name is <u>Willis</u>.

14. Her favorite <u>author</u> is <u>A. A. Milne</u>.

15. Her <u>neighbor</u>, <u>Marcia Thomas</u>, likes to jog in the morning.

16. My best friend's <u>first name</u>, <u>middle initial</u>, and <u>last name</u> are <u>Ronald J. Samuelson</u>.

17. She decided to name her pet <u>dog</u> <u>Flash</u>.

18. When he sang, he sounded like the famous <u>singer</u> <u>Pavarotti</u>.

19. One afternoon, she met the popular <u>actress</u> <u>Geena Davis</u>.

20. The first <u>U.S. president</u> that comes to mind is <u>George Washington</u>.

### Capitalization C, pp. 109–10
#### EXERCISE A
1. My closest relatives live in (P)asadena.

2. One of his cousins went snorkeling near the Great Barrier Reef.

3. Any animal that can survive the weather in Antarctica deserves to be studied.

4. We should visit Grasslands National Park someday.

5. Peru is a country located in South America.

6. This book contains a picture of the Rock of Gibraltar.

7. Each fall, our town holds a festival on Lucinda Avenue.

8. We can only marvel at the length of the Colorado River.

9. She dreams of living close to the beaches in Hawaii.

10. The band marched up Fourth Street, and then headed down Fifth.

**EXERCISE B**
11. **a.** Eastvale Falcons
12. **b.** New York Court of Appeals
13. **b.** Metropolitan Museum of Art
14. **a.** United States Senate
15. **b.** University of Southern California

**EXERCISE C**
16. Making laws in the United States is complicated, and the governmental body called the House of Representatives is a big part of that process.

17. The Krishna River is a river that flows in the southern part of India.

18. Did Aunt Jessie see many different kinds of birds as she drove through Klamath National Forest in California?

19. When she gets older, Myra wants to play basketball for the University of Texas Longhorns.

20. Have you seen a picture of the Sydney Opera House, that famous building in Australia?

## Capitalization D, pp. 111–12
**EXERCISE A**
1. The day we now call Presidents' Day used to be called Washington's Birthday.

2. The scientists discovered a dinosaur bone from the Jurassic Era.

3. Will we have a picnic to celebrate the Fourth of July?

4. The season of spring begins in March.

5. At the end of January, Lee's family always celebrates the festival called Tet.

6. During the parade on Arbor Day, he rode on a float shaped like a tree.

7. She dreams that she will one day be able to play in the World Series.

8. I think our trip should be on a Saturday.

9. Sheila said that today was the holiday Purim.

10. Many forms of art began to flourish during the Renaissance.

**EXERCISE B**
11. **b.** African Americans
12. **a.** an Asian
13. **b.** the Greeks
14. **b.** a Bantu
15. **a.** American Indians

**EXERCISE C**
*Answers will vary. Sample responses are provided.*

16. My aunt flies a small <u>plane</u> she named ___Gnatt___.

17. Her mother works for ___Happy Days___, a <u>business</u> that designs greeting cards.

18. We took a <u>train</u> ride aboard ___the General___, an old steam-driven locomotive.

**19.** The <u>space shuttle</u> __Endeavour__ has docked with the International Space Station.

**20.** I usually write with a __Bic__ , my favorite <u>brand</u> of pen.

## Capitalization E, pp. 113–14

**EXERCISE A**

**1.** When Clara toured San Francisco, she took pictures of the Ⓖolden Ⓖate Ⓑridge.

**2.** Someday, the Ⓟulitzer Prize is going to go to my next-door neighbor.

**3.** He really deserves an Ⓞscar for his performance after school.

**4.** Our teacher said that he wanted to stand at the base of the Ⓔmpire Ⓢtate Ⓑuilding and look straight upward.

**5.** Alex and Justin counted all of the steps leading to the top of the Ⓢtatue of Ⓛiberty.

**EXERCISE B**

**6.** The hero of the story was lost at sea because he angered the god Ⓟoseidon.

**7.** What is the name of the first book of the Ⓑible?

**8.** Because his family observes the holy days of Ⓡamadan, he and his brother are fasting from dawn to sunset.

**9.** As the famous Ⓑuddhist began to explain his spiritual beliefs, the audience grew quiet.

**10.** Christians everywhere will celebrate Ⓔaster very soon.

**EXERCISE C**

*Answers will vary. Sample responses are provided.*

**11.** On a clear, light-free night, the <u>galaxy</u> __Andromeda__ is visible.

**12.** Mike thought he saw a UFO, but it was really just the <u>planet</u> __Venus__ .

**13.** My favorite <u>constellation</u> is __Orion__ because it is so easy to spot.

**14.** That <u>comet</u>, called __Halley's Comet__ , is an immense pool of interstellar gas.

**15.** The small-looking <u>star</u> __Polaris__ guided explorers as they traveled.

## Capitalization F, pp. 115–16

**EXERCISE A**

**1. b.** Civics 101

**2. a.** Geology 3300

**3. b.** Creative Writing 2

**4. a.** English

**5. a.** Physics 1

**EXERCISE B**

**6.** Some high school students will take Ⓒhemistry.

**7.** Next Saturday there will be a class for mountain bikers, Bicycle Ⓜaintenance I, at the school.

**8.** I wonder what will be taught in the community class called Conversational Ⓙapanese III.

**9.** Will Jamal be taking Ⓙournalism 101 during his first year of high school?

**10.** Mrs. Tanaka will be teaching the summer-camp class called Ⓢpanish for Ⓑeginners.

**EXERCISE C**

**11.** The Ⓐlaskan landscape is home to bears, whales, and moose.

**12.** Tessa is studying Ⓡoman architecture at the local community college.

**13.** A Ⓢcottish bagpipe player is on the cover of that book about music in Scotland.

**14.** Because the Arctic is such a cold place, I have always admired the endurance of Ⓐrctic animals.

15. Our neighbors, who want to visit Portugal one day, collect (P)ortuguese sculpture.

16. Have you noticed that this restaurant has a (H)ollywood theme?

17. Her hockey team's only (C)anadian player is an especially fast skater.

18. Using the (J)apanese tea garden as a backdrop, the photographer snapped many shots.

19. Rosa wears the most beautiful (S)panish dresses.

20. Prepare yourself for another (M)innesotan winter.

## Capitalization G, pp. 117–18

### EXERCISE A

1. The man who teaches my weekend computer class is named (P)rofessor Cho.

2. I am reading an interesting article on the life of (E)mperor Augustus.

3. He probably never dreamed that one day he would be known as (S)ir Paul McCartney.

4. My favorite justice has always been (J)ustice Potter Stewart.

5. One of our country's least popular presidents may have been (P)resident Millard Fillmore.

6. She spoke with (D)eacon Callison about the grand opening of the new park.

7. According to (S)enator Hawley, getting elected is far more difficult than serving in office.

8. Using cowpox germs, (S)ir Edward Jenner developed a vaccination for smallpox.

9. The first professional woman astronomer in the United States was (P)rofessor Maria Mitchell.

10. Our class met briefly with (R)abbi Goldmann.

### EXERCISE B

11. **b.** "What Is Enlightenment?"

12. **b.** "Finding the Right Sunscreen"

13. **a.** "Mother to Son"

14. **a.** *Mona Lisa*

15. **b.** *Rhapsody in Blue*

### EXERCISE C

16. Carrie's copy of the book *A Walk (I)n the (W)oods* has a photo of a bear on the cover.

17. What is the topic of that article, "Bravery in an (U)nexpected Place," that Ruben is reading?

18. The bright blues, reds, and yellows in the collage *Harriet Tubman (A)nd (T)he Freedom Train* make this lively piece of artwork noticeable.

19. The movie *Father (O)f the (B)ride* made my dad laugh.

20. The Miles Davis CD called *Kind (O)f (B)lue* has jazz performances that include saxophone, piano, bass, and drums.

## Chapter 11: Punctuation, pp. 119–128

### End Marks and Abbreviations, pp. 119–120

**EXERCISE A**

1. Did Jared forget his lunch?
2. Have you washed and vacuumed the car?
3. Debra is going to keep a snowball in her freezer.
4. He wondered when the rain would stop.
5. What did the puppy just do?

**EXERCISE B**

6. What movie are you seeing tonight?
7. Shoot the ball now!
8. That concert was incredibly exciting!
9. Please help me clear the table.
10. She was wondering whether we would help move the sofa.

**EXERCISE C**

11. Dr. Truman
12. J. R. R. Tolkien
13. Mrs. Jackson
14. Judy Stone, D. D. S.
15. 108 West Oak St.
16. Frank Salazar, Jr.
17. San Diego, Calif.
18. 1423 S. First St.
19. A. D. 1066
20. New York, N. Y.

### Commas with Items in a Series, pp. 121–122

**EXERCISE A**

1. Grandmother photographs family events, prepares a scrapbook for each grandchild, keeps a journal of vacation trips, and attends most of our games.
2. Put the tomato plants, the bags of mulch, the hose, and the small shovel into the wheelbarrow.
3. The musicians could be heard in the yard, in the garden, and throughout the house.
4. C
5. Alexandra, Maria, Kimi, and Andrea are moving to new desks.

6. Lightning flashed, thunder boomed, the wind howled, and rain pelted the windows.
7. Crickets will chirp, rustle around in the dry leaves, hop from corner to corner, and sing through the night.
8. C
9. In the yard were four lawn chairs, two tables, and one open umbrella.
10. C

**EXERCISE B**

11. a
12. b
13. b
14. a
15. a

### Commas with Independent Clauses, pp. 123–124

**EXERCISE A**

1. b
2. a
3. b
4. a
5. b

**EXERCISE B**

6. Most young adults enjoy music, yet they dislike certain songs.
7. C
8. Many people can't sing well, but they can play an instrument.
9. C
10. C
11. Vocal music may not help learning, for the lyrics can interfere with concentration.
12. C
13. They enjoy music, but they also find music distracting.
14. Some classical music may improve test scores, yet rock music can decrease them.
15. Each person is different, so you must choose your own study routine.

## Commas with Introductory Elements, pp. 125–126

**EXERCISE A**

1. Hey, is that a dollar bill stuck to your shoe?

2. Swallowing nervously, Carl wiped his sweaty hands on his jeans.

3. *C*

4. My, this has been an exciting first day.

5. Raising her arms, the vice-presidential nominee predicted victory.

6. Sure, there are a few bugs in the software program.

7. Locked into our old views about eating, how can we improve our diet?

8. *C*

9. Thinking of a dozen topics, Wynnie couldn't decide where to begin her research.

10. Yes, isn't that the most interesting painting in the exhibit?

**EXERCISE B**

11. Behind the poster of a buffalo, you will find a wall safe.

12. *C*

13. When it is locked, the safe is almost impossible to crack.

14. In addition to that, we can't forget where we've hidden the key.

15. *C*

16. Although our sister didn't like the choice, we knew what to do.

17. Since we didn't want to forget where we hid it, we decided to keep the key nearby.

18. Against our sister's repeated advice, we hid the key on the back of the poster.

19. With all of her objections, you'd think that we'd left the key in plain sight.

20. If she doesn't understand our reasoning about hiding places, she can hide her valuables somewhere else.

## Commas with Interrupters, pp. 127–128

**EXERCISE A**

1. b
2. b
3. a
4. b
5. a
6. b
7. a
8. a
9. b
10. a

**EXERCISE B**

11. Recycling, generally speaking, is good for the environment.

12. Could this be a case of mistaken identity, Maria?

13. My cat, Smudge, would never have climbed into Dad's new car.

14. That, nevertheless, is exactly where I found him.

15. Pablo Picasso, the world-renowned artist, still has thousands of admirers today.

16. The game, consequently, will have to be rescheduled.

17. *C*

18. *C*

19. According to the latest survey, the election will be very close.

20. *C*

## Chapter 12: Punctuation, pp. 129–132

### Semicolons, pp. 129–130

**Exercise A**

_____ **1.** The western sky has reddened; the sun will set within the hour.

_____ **2.** Beth has finished assembling her solar lawn mower; however, the blades still need to be balanced.

_____ **3.** It is getting easier to find many forms of wildlife; indeed, even the bald eagle is becoming more common.

__C__ **4.** Her aunt gave her some potted violets, so she is learning how to grow them.

_____ **5.** He's eating fresh cantaloupe; where did he find it?

_____ **6.** There are empty boxes stacked in the hallway; we should probably recycle them.

__C__ **7.** Comets are difficult to discover, yet Dr. Rhodes keeps trying to find one.

_____ **8.** Carl's books, papers, and pencils are already lying on the table in the kitchen; in other words, our study group is going to meet there.

_____ **9.** To reach the doctor's office, go to the fourth floor; the office will be on your left.

_____ **10.** The bridge is usually busy with traffic; nevertheless, pigeons nest below it.

**Exercise B**

__C__ **11.** Unlike nonliving things, living things move on their own, respond to changes in condition, consume nutrients, and grow and replace parts.

_____ **12.** On their whirlwind tour of the East, the retirees will visit Orlando, Florida; Richmond, Virginia; and Boston, Massachusetts.

_____ **13.** Three of Oklahoma's natural regions are the Gulf Coastal Plain, a fertile region that spreads along the valley of the Red River; the Ouachita Mountains, a forested area that extends into western Arkansas; and the Central Plains, a grassland prairie that forms the largest region in the state.

_____ **14.** A spokesperson for the San Gabriel Community Center said that they can host the "Build a Better Mousetrap" competition on November 16 or 23, 2004; December 12 or 29, 2004; January 6 or 23, 2005; or February 9 or 16, 2005.

_____ **15.** Artificial turf doesn't require much care, isn't easily damaged, and is unaffected by weather; but its use may lead to certain injuries, cause balls to bounce higher than they would on a natural surface, and raise field temperatures in warm weather.

## Colons, pp. 131–132

1. Do not forget to bring the following materials: entry fees, all photographs and artwork, display stands, a display table, a comfortable chair or stool, a list of prices for any artwork offered for sale, and a calculator.

2. Our treasurer reminded us: "we must act before it is too late. We must respond to the demands of the current situation. If we are to avoid a financial crisis that might put us out of business altogether, all new members need to get their dues in to their team leaders within two days."

3. We will need these supplies: six fresh cans of paint, three paintbrushes, two paint rollers, a pair of paint trays, a protective sheet, a small ladder, masking tape, and old clothes.

4. Additional recommendations are as follows: decrease expenses and levels of absenteeism, and improve production efficiencies and levels of sales.

5. In a speech delivered to this year's graduates, she said: "the diploma you'll receive today is far more than a piece of paper. It is, instead, a symbol of triumph. It is a symbol of determination and dedication to success. Indeed, when you finally hold the diploma you are about to receive, remember that it is not a piece of paper. It is a flag you are receiving. A flag dedicated to victory."

**EXERCISE B**

6. Sometime between 8:16 A.M. and 8:19 A.M. teachers will announce the results of last week's election.

7. *Elements of Literature: Third Course*

8. Pharaoh's daughter, in Exodus 2:6, feels sorry for the baby she's found.

9. Our flight departs at 5:55 A.M.

10. Dear Dr. Delgado:

## Chapter 13: Punctuation, pp. 133–138
### Italics (Underlining), pp. 133–134
**EXERCISE A**

1. Has Jane Austen's book <u>Pride and Prejudice</u> ever been made into a movie?

2. One of Donatello's marble sculptures, <u>St. George</u>, depicts human self-confidence.

3. William Shakespeare wrote <u>Romeo and Juliet</u>.

4. Someone sent a long letter to <u>The Middlevale Gazette</u> saying that its editorials were too long.

5. We have a recording of <u>Amahl and the Night Visitors</u>, the first opera written for television.

6. The movie <u>Apollo 13</u> is about events that happened before I was born.

7. No one knows who wrote <u>Beowulf</u>, the epic poem.

8. Georgia O'Keeffe's artistic style is displayed in her painting <u>Black Iris</u>.

9. Dr. Seuss once worked as an illustrator and humorist for the magazine <u>Life</u>.

10. Some of Nathaniel Hawthorne's stories were collected in the book <u>Twice-Told Tales</u>.

**EXERCISE B**

11. My whole family once got up early enough to see the space station <u>Mir</u> pass overhead.

12. Paul is fascinated with the battle between <u>Merrimack</u> and <u>Monitor</u>, two ironclad ships used during the Civil War.

13. Didn't the first U.S. space satellite, <u>Explorer 1</u>, discover charged particles surrounding Earth?

14. Like several other lighter-than-air aircraft, the <u>Shenandoah</u> couldn't withstand poor weather.

15. The Chisholms aren't here because they're taking a train trip aboard the <u>Kentucky Flyer</u>.

**EXERCISE C**

16. She told him not to worry because it was only an <u>igel</u>, or, as she explained, a hedgehog.

17. Be certain to use the <u>¶</u> mark to indicate where your paragraphs should begin.

18. In French, the two words for "personal computer" are <u>ordinateur personnel</u>.

19. His handwriting is hard to read, but it looks like he wrote down a <u>93</u> as his best golf score.

20. The <u>£</u> symbol looks odd to us, but it stands for "pound," an English unit of currency.

### Quotation Marks A, pp. 135–136
**EXERCISE A**

1. "Hold on a minute!" Lani hollered.

2. The electrician said, "go ahead and flip the circuit breakers back on."

3. "Do you think we can climb over all of those hills in just one afternoon?" said Audrey.

4. Jesse grabbed a sweater, swung the walk-in cooler's door open, and mumbled, "it's chilly in there."

5. She explained, "you'll get there if you turn right on Bleaker and then walk one block."

6. Rosa wondered aloud, "Should I go upstairs or stay down here?"

7. "I can't go. You know I have to visit my cousins," Crystal told us.

8. "Run to second base!" yelled the coach.

9. I heard someone shout, "don't forget to close the door!"

10. "can you believe this weather?" Len asked with a smile.

**EXERCISE B**

11. "I think I'd rather be walking," she said, "than waiting to go for a walk."

12. "The only problem," he grinned, "is that we don't have a car."

13. "Little man, always be polite!" My grandmother used to say.

14. "All leaders should line up at noon," the memo read, "so don't be late!"

15. "Step right up," the carnival worker teased, "And try your luck!"

16. She wondered, "is this the only map we have?" as she gazed at the tattered page.

17. The coach bellowed, "Listen up!" once the team was seated.

18. "I," he sighed beside us on the plane, "hear a baby cooing in the seats behind us."

19. "Your curiosity," Ms. Carvel whispered to her daughters, "is a gift."

20. "We have a guest," our teacher told us, "Visiting this morning."

**Quotation Marks B, pp. 137–138**

**EXERCISE A**

1. In his article "How Insects Learned to Fly," James H. Marden discusses early insects and how they first began to fly.

2. His grandfather is always whistling the chorus to the song "When I'm Sixty Four."

3. Her parents first fell in love when they both agreed that "The Trouble with Tribbles" was the best episode of that old show.

4. In English class, we've been talking about Guy de Maupassant's short story "The Necklace."

5. Is "The Washwoman" a first-person short story, or is it an autobiographical essay?

6. On the bus, her brother and his friends sang "The Ants Go Marching" for most of the day.

7. The poem "The Lesson of the Moth" is supposed to have been written by a cockroach.

8. I'm sure that she said to read the chapter "Sharing an Opinion."

9. Believe it or not, after following the instructions in the chapter "Using Brochures," Jody created a brochure that convinced his parents to take a family vacation.

10. Roald Dahl's story about a man who thinks a snake is sleeping on his stomach, "Poison," is really an attack on racist thinking.

**EXERCISE B**
*Answers will vary. Sample responses are provided.*

11. ___"Fog"___ is a poem suited to the discussions we've been having.

12. I've already finished reading ___"The Ways We Are___," which is a chapter in our textbook.

13. We really enjoyed the article titled ___"It's OK to Be Different___."

14. How in the world did you memorize the poem ___"The Gift"___ so quickly?

**15.** ___"Harrison Bergeron"___ is a <u>short story</u> meant to tell us a great deal about the central character's strengths.

**16.** The <u>essay</u> ___"New Directions"___ encourages people to take a positive view of the future.

**17.** Have you heard the <u>song</u> ___"Calypso"___ yet?

**18.** On the Internet, I found an <u>article</u> called ___"Fueling the Wonder"___ about subway systems.

**19.** Tonight's <u>television episode</u>, ___"Apples and Onions___," will surely draw a large audience.

**20.** Have any of you read the <u>short story</u> ___"Marigolds"___?

# Chapter 14: Punctuation, pp. 139–140

**Apostrophes, pp. 139–140**

**EXERCISE A**

1. Penicillin's
2. Lampasas'
3. glass's
4. Bedford's
5. hippopotamus's

**EXERCISE B**

6. bosses', theirs
7. herons', its
8. women's, neither's
9. ties', his
10. delegates', everyone's

**EXERCISE C**

11. Shouldn't we tell them that they're supposed to use *a*'s and *b*'s rather than *1*'s and *2*'s in their outlines?

12. Mike's agreeing that he'd prefer to get to class at nine o'clock.

13. You're definitely going to get *A*'s if your study habits don't change.

14. Back in '49, after studying this creek, she predicted that we'd eventually discover gold here.

15. If we are going to finish this project on time, it's easy to see that we're going to need to remove some of the *don't*'s and *won't*'s from our vocabularies.

# Chapter 15: Punctuation, pp. 141–44

## Hyphens and Ellipses, pp. 141–42

### EXERCISE A

*Answers, save items 3 and 4, may vary according to the dictionary used.*

1. Ne-pal
2. Broad-way
3. C
4. C
5. holo-graph

### EXERCISE B

6. The formula calls for one‸half ounce acetic acid.
7. Tyrone's score on this game may be an all‸time high.
8. Some pre‸Socratic philosophers thought the universe was made of water.
9. At least forty‸five bearings are inside this wheel's hub.
10. Isn't she an ex‸member of the debating team.

### EXERCISE C

11. The center stands on three acres of woodland, and it houses sixteen injured birds. *(# . # . # . #)*
12. People often find downed birds and bring them to the center. *(. # . # . #)*
13. Our biggest success was with a golden eagle that we released this fall. *(. # . # .)*
14. Her first fuzz-covered eaglet has just hatched. *(# . # . # . #)*
15. It's almost ready to fly alongside its parents and other eagles because its regular feathers have begun to grow. *(# . # . # . #)*

## Parentheses, Dashes, and Brackets, pp. 143–144

### EXERCISE A

1. The Empire State Building (located on Fifth Avenue) was completed in 1931.
2. George Eliot (1819–1880) is the pen name of the novelist Mary Ann Evans.
3. By December 15, 1791, the Bill of Rights (the first ten amendments to the Constitution) had been approved by a sufficient number of states.
4. Mark Twain (Samuel Langhorne Clemens) wrote *Life on the Mississippi.*
5. *When I Was Young in the Mountains* (1982) is a book about Cynthia Rylant's childhood in West Virginia.

### EXERCISE B

6. Their ancestral homes—small mud and straw buildings—eroded into dust long ago.
7. Sheila's little sister—she's only seven years old—is already studying algebra.
8. The Aztecs' principal food consisted of cornmeal pancakes—tortillas.
9. "So when is this roller coaster going to take—" he said, and then he shrieked.
10. The Taj Mahal—one of the most expensive tombs ever built—was constructed in memory of an Indian ruler's wife.

### EXERCISE C

*Answers will vary. Suggested responses follow.*

11. The Board of Directors announced, "We are happy that all of our new stores will be operational soon __[July]__, and we are pleased by increased growth." *(the name of a month)*

**12.** "The main character ___[Buddy]___ often agrees with the nation's value system," he explained. *(a character's name)*

**13.** "While we all knew who would win the student assembly seat ___[Kim]___, we hadn't expected it to be by such a large margin." *(the name of the winner)*

**14.** I hope that this letter (and the enclosed materials ___[flyers for distribution]___) have arrived safely. *(a description of the enclosed materials)*

**15.** He tells us, "According to her book, they ___[giant squid]___ have never been seen alive in their deep-sea home." *(a type of sea animal)*

## Chapter 16: Spelling, pp. 145–56
### Words with *ie* and *ei,* pp. 145–46
EXERCISE A

1. deceit
2. interview
3. cashiers
4. neighbors'
5. briefcase
6. pier
7. pieces
8. view
9. forfeit
10. beliefs

EXERCISE B

11. achieved
12. foreign
13. veins
14. mischief
15. weights
16. brief
17. received
18. Their
19. believe
20. receipt

### Prefixes and Suffixes, pp. 147–48
EXERCISE A

1. preview
2. uneventful
3. impatient
4. misunderstand
5. reorganize

EXERCISE B

6. bluish
7. timeless
8. aging
9. peaceful
10. baked

EXERCISE C

11. **a.** enjoyment
12. **b.** loneliness

13. **b.** reliable
14. **a.** saying
15. **b.** likelihood

EXERCISE D

16. beginning
17. regrettable
18. keeper
19. topped
20. dented

### Plurals of Nouns, pp. 149–50
EXERCISE A

1. passengers
2. boxes
3. dishes
4. Jordans
5. finches
6. cables
7. flowers
8. benches
9. lurches
10. faxes

EXERCISE B

11. women
12. enemies
13. selves
14. moose
15. tragedies
16. thieves
17. allies
18. wolves
19. children
20. shelves

EXERCISE C

21. &'s
22. 17's
23. i's
24. that's
25. $'s

## Words Often Confused A, pp. 151–52

**EXERCISE A**

1. altogether
2. all ready
3. effect
4. already
5. all ready
6. already
7. affect
8. all together
9. affect
10. all together

**EXERCISE B**

11. chose
12. brakes
13. choose
14. break
15. choose
16. brake
17. breaks
18. choose
19. brakes
20. chose

## Words Often Confused B, pp. 153–54

**EXERCISE A**

1. Here
2. deserts
3. dessert
4. course
5. coarse
6. desert
7. course
8. here
9. course
10. hear

**EXERCISE B**

11. lead
12. its
13. it's
14. led
15. its
16. it's
17. led
18. lead
19. lead
20. lead

## Words Often Confused C, pp. 155–56

**EXERCISE A**

1. piece
2. peace
3. quiet
4. past
5. passed

**EXERCISE B**

6. too
7. There
8. two
9. to
10. there
11. to
12. They're
13. too
14. their
15. too

## Chapter 17: Correcting Common Errors, pp. 157–58

**Common Errors Review, pp. 157–58**

### EXERCISE A

*Some answers may vary.*

1. Sandra and Martin built their first garden in Sandra's backyard, but ~~it~~ they ran out of room so they ~~find~~ found a new plot in the city's garden area.

2. Looking for new kinds of vegetable~~s~~ to grow, ~~seed catalogs are read quickly by the two.~~ the two quickly read seed catalogs

3. They try ~~and~~ to raise new varieties every year, and they do all of the gardening themselves.

4. ~~Her~~ She and Martin plant carrots, radishes, and lettuce early in the season.

5. During last spring's cooler~~st~~ weeks, Martin, for who~~m~~ tomatoes are a treat, bought tomato plants and stakes at a local nursery.

6. Sandra and ~~him go~~ he went to plant the tomatoes, but they found that they still had work to do.

7. [Sprouting from the well-tilled soil, they found weeds,] but neither teen ~~would~~ wanted to pull them.

8. Luckily, two nearby gardeners said that they ~~will~~ would help, if, once they finished weeding Sandra and Martin's garden, Sandra and Martin ~~was~~ were to help them in return.

9. Sandra and Martin, when their own garden ~~was~~ finished, helped their new friends plant vegetables for ~~theirselves.~~ themselves.

10. Martin and Sandra now garden very ~~good,~~ well, especially after having got~~ten~~ so much practice.

### EXERCISE B

*Some answers may vary.*

11. Some people believe that Duke paoa kahanamoku, the winner of three Olympic gold medals, was the world's best freestyle swimmer.

12. He won gold medals in 100-meter freestyle events in stockholm (1912) and Antwerp (1920), and he was a member of the winning United states team in the 800-meter relay.

13. Didn't he take his ten-foot surfboard with him whenever he traveled outside Hawaii?

14. "I am only happy," he once said, "When I am swimming like a fish."

15. He had a worldwide ~~affect~~ effect on the sport; by the time of Duke's death, surfing had become ~~quiet~~ quite popular all over the world.

## Chapter 18: Complete Sentences, pp. 159–162

### Complete Sentences and Sentence Fragments, pp. 159–160

**EXERCISE A**

1. S
2. N
3. V
4. N
5. S (*or* V)

**EXERCISE B**

*Answers will vary. Sample responses are given.*

6. The bats were hungry for their dinner of insects.
7. I was sitting near a cave when I wrote the story about the bats.
8. I did not go inside the dark, spooky cave.
9. The bats, which slept during the daylight hours, came out at night.
10. They are small brownish-black animals.

### Run-on Sentences, pp. 161–162

**EXERCISE A**

1. R
2. C
3. C
4. R
5. R

**EXERCISE B**

*Answers will vary. Sample responses are given.*

6. Chad sings in a country western band. He is my cousin.
7. We studied for the test together; therefore, we had confidence during the exam.
8. Write down your e-mail address for me, or write down your phone number.
9. In the pigpen, the pigs rolled in mud. I wondered if they felt happy.
10. Each day I walk to school, for the distance is only half a mile.

Copyright © by Holt, Rinehart and Winston. All rights reserved.

**40**

HOLT HANDBOOK | Third Course

## Chapter 19: Combining Sentences, pp. 163–176

### Combining Sentences by Inserting Words and Phrases, pp. 163–164

**EXERCISE A**

*Placement of adverbs in items 1, 3, and 5, and of adjectives in item 2 may vary.*

1. The students eagerly attend shop class each day.
2. Joe built a large, sturdy cedar chest.
3. In shop class, Brad skillfully built a chair.
4. Did you see Melanie's small birdhouse?
5. For weeks, she carefully worked on the birdhouse.

**EXERCISE B**

*Answers may vary.*

6. Swinging from tree to tree, the monkey moved through the forest.
7. Hungrily, the monkey searched for birds' eggs.
8. Did you see the monkey, an old male, that is the head of its clan?
9. Grabbed by a spider monkey, the piece of cantaloupe is gone.
10. Listen to that noisy one, a howler monkey.

### Combining Sentences Using Coordinating Conjunctions, pp. 165–166

**EXERCISE A**

*Answers may vary.*

1. Kim sits and waits quietly at the subway station.
2. Men and women patiently check their watches and tap their feet nervously.
3. Newsstands and vendors are nearby.
4. Passengers sit and stand in the train.
5. The cars and passengers rock from side to side and sway together.

**EXERCISE B**

*Answers may vary.*

6. Captain Kidd became a famous pirate in English literature; however, Blackbeard became a famous pirate in American folklore.
7. At first, Captain Kidd hunted pirates, but he later became a pirate himself.
8. Blackbeard is the nickname of another pirate; Edward Teach was his name.
9. Blackbeard patrolled the Caribbean Sea, and he eluded capture for at least two years.
10. Eventually Blackbeard was killed; nevertheless, his legendary treasure was never found.

### Combining Sentences Using Subordinate Clauses, pp. 167–168

**EXERCISE A**

*Answers may vary.*

1. Please introduce me to the girl who painted that mural.
2. The hinge that squeaks needs oil.
3. Cherry yogurt, which makes a good dessert, is on the menu.
4. Yesterday, a few volunteers who were at hand moved Mr. Soto's furniture.
5. Did you notice the full moon that was in the sky last night?

**EXERCISE B**

*Answers may vary.*

6. That Jessi asked me to the dance made me happy.
7. After it rained heavily last night, the creek's water level rose almost six inches.
8. That you knew the answer did not surprise me.
9. Because lemurs move in a quiet, ghostlike fashion, their name, *lemur*, was taken from a Latin word that means "ghosts."
10. If you teach me about horses, I'll teach you about saddles.

### Revising for Parallelism, pp. 169–170

**EXERCISE A**

1. P
2. N
3. P
4. N
5. N

**EXERCISE B**

*Answers may vary.*

**6.** Steve is a member of the yearbook staff, the choir, and ~~he plays on~~ the golf team.

**7.** The lizard saw that a flower had opened and that insects were inside it.

**8.** In her backpack Sandra carries books, papers, and ~~there are~~ snacks.

**9.** Were they searching under the bridge, beside the river, and in the forest?

**10.** Give your phone number only to someone whom you know and ~~trustworthy~~ whom you trust.

**EXERCISE C**

*Answers may vary.*

**11.** After school, I do homework, I clean my room, and I cook dinner.

**12.** The trees grew tall, green, and wide.

**13.** Did you search on the Internet, in an encyclopedia, and in the textbook?

**14.** Teach me to design a bookcase and to build it.

**15.** Suddenly he realized that he had overslept and that he was late.

## Revising Stringy Sentences, pp. 171–172

**EXERCISE A**

1. SS
2. N
3. SS
4. SS
5. SS

**EXERCISE B**

*Answers will vary.*

**6.** Donna called me on Friday, ~~and~~ my mom took a message, but she didn't give me the message until Sunday. When ~~and~~ I called Donna, ~~but~~ she thought I had ignored her.

**7.** During lunch we were looking at fashion magazines ~~and we studied~~ studying the pictures of prom dresses. Although ~~but~~ we can't afford any of them, ~~but~~ Lisa can sew them herself.

**8.** When ~~and~~ I was selling candy for band, ~~and~~ I rang a doorbell, but no one answered. ~~and~~ I walked away, but then someone opened the door and called to me.

**9.** For Valentine's Day I write poems ~~and they are~~ for friends, ~~and then~~ I make cards. ~~and~~ I copy the poems inside, ~~and~~ my friends like them.

**10.** Kyle opened the door, and a gust of wind blew the door, ~~and~~ hitting the door flew out of his hand, ~~and it hit~~ where the wall, ~~and~~ the doorknob made a hole, ~~and the hole was in the wall.~~

## Revising Wordy Sentences, pp. 173–174

**EXERCISE A**

1. W
2. W
3. N
4. N
5. W

**EXERCISE B**

*Answers will vary.*

**6.** While I studied, I continually ate peanuts.

**7.** If they follow the rules, they should be allowed to use the pool.

**8.** We will carry out the plan and record the results.

**9.** C

**10.** The oak table was skillfully constructed.

**11.** Is each student in this class ready to start the algebra lesson?

**12.** C

**13.** Although it was sunny, the day stayed cool.

**14.** After the swim meet, she wore a happy expression.

**15.** These facts are in the encyclopedia.

**Varying Sentence Beginnings, pp. 175–176**

EXERCISE A

*Answers may vary.*

1. Looking through a telescope, Holly saw the planet Venus.
2. Shrilly, the telephone in the hall rang.
3. Beside the fireplace, the dog and her puppies slept.
4. To get closer to home plate, James stole third base.
5. Feeling creative, Sasha wrote in her journal.

EXERCISE B

*Answers will vary.*

6. Although George is short, he is good at basketball.
7. After the lake's surface had calmed, the wind caused it to ripple again.
8. Because the day was rainy, the dog did not go outside.
9. When the fire alarm went off, I jumped out of my seat.
10. Where the snow had melted, new grass was growing.

## Resources, pp. 177–78

### Manuscript Form, pp. 177–78

Students should have transferred information given in the exercise to the appropriate lines on the model page.